A Glimpse Into God's Heart

A Glimpse Into God's Heart

Learning Forgiveness From the Father

By Kirk Brothers

Gospel Advocate Company

Nashville, Tennessee

Published by Gospel Advocate Co.
1006 Elm Hill Pike, Nashville, TN 37210
http://www.gospeladvocate.com

ISBN: 0-89225-553-6

Dedication

I dedicate this book to my wife, Cindy (Markham), my daughters, Katie and Hannah, and my parents, Joe and Dorothy Brothers. They have given me a glimpse of the heart of God.

Acknowledgments

I would like to thank Marion Pistole, Matthew Winkler, Cindy Brothers, Beverly Ramsey, Traci Jones, Lane Dix and David Wright for their suggestions and/or help in editing portions of this material.

I appreciate Lori Boyd and Connie Riddle for printing the congregational versions of this book.

I am indebted to the members of Central Church of Christ and the Graymere Church of Christ for their input and support during the writing and teaching of this material and for their constant love.

I thank Mike Matheny for overseeing the practicum which included the writing of this book. The fact that these people played various rolls in the production of the manuscript does not necessarily mean that they agree with every statement in the book.

I am eternally thankful to my sisters and brother (Renee, Tracy, T.J., Jason), many relatives, brothers and sisters in Christ, Bible class teachers and college professors who have taught me by word and deed about the forgiveness of God.

Most of all, I thank my God for providing the subject matter for this study. Without Jesus Christ, this book would be pointless. Thank You, Father, for showing us Your heart!

Table of Contents

Introduction

We all have skeletons in our spiritual closets (Romans 3:23), and sometimes they come out and occupy our minds. I am haunted by the ghosts of all the sins I have committed in my life. I struggle with letting go of my guilt, and this book is part of my personal investigation of God's Word to find peace.

Many of my fellow Christians also are haunted. Congregations are not immune to situations that involve forgiveness: the murder or accidental death of a child, a mother killed by a drunk driver, an abusive parent, an alcoholic spouse, and infighting among members.

I do "sermon surveys" at the congregations I work with to learn what topics the members would like me to explore in my sermons. Forgiveness frequently fills those survey responses: After praying for forgiveness for sins of the past, can we be sure we are forgiven? Why is it so hard to forget after we forgive? Does one sin condemn one to hell? Who deserves to get into heaven? How does one learn to forgive fully and put hurts behind?

Planting and Watering a Seed

The writing of this book was further influenced by two speaking assignments and an informal comment. I was asked to do a lesson on Matthew 18 for a local Vacation Bible School and a lesson on Colossians

1:14 for the Freed-Hardeman University Lectures. I found these to be enriching and complementary studies. A publisher mentioned on a couple of occasions that he would like for someone to write a book on forgiveness. He felt there was a tremendous need for it. He didn't realize it, but he planted a seed that began to germinate in my mind.

I started choosing projects and assignments in my graduate classes that would allow me to do in-depth study of the subject. I spent over a year scouring the more than 200 passages on forgiveness in the Bible. I researched the relevant Hebrew and Greek terms. Most importantly, I put emphasis on the overall message of the entire Bible. What is God trying to say to us and how does the subject of forgiveness relate to it? I was reminded that forgiveness is at the heart of the biblical story and that it gives us a glimpse into God's heart.

I wondered if an extensive study of forgiveness would be relevant to the needs of the congregation I was working with at the time. I suddenly found myself confronted with several forgiveness situations within the congregation. They seemed to come out of the woodwork, many involving conflicts that had gone unresolved for years. I then gave a survey to the congregation on a Wednesday night. I asked the teenagers and all four adult classes to respond to seven questions:

1. What is your age bracket?

2. Have you been baptized into Christ for the forgiveness of your sins?

3. How long have you been a Christian?

4. How often do you attend Bible class and/or worship?

5. How often do you read your Bible per week outside of Bible class and worship?

6. How often do you pray each day or week outside of Bible class and worship?

7. If you died right now, would you go to heaven?

The survey confirmed the need for the study. Responses came from 167 teens and adults. The results were troubling. The key question was, "If you died right now, would you go to heaven?" There were four choices: (1) Yes; (2) No; (3) I don't know; and (4) I think so, but I am not sure. In a group of respondents who were among the most active and committed members, 94 percent claiming to be Christians, 38 percent gave one of the three negative answers. They could not say that they knew they were going to heaven. Of the teens who responded, 74 percent claimed to be Christians but only 26 percent were confident in their salvation. Amazingly, 37 percent of those in the 65 and up age group could not say they were going to heaven. These senior saints averaged 51 years of experience as a Christian.

I also learned from the same survey that a few people who had not been baptized thought they were going to heaven. Several who never prayed or read their Bible thought they were going to heaven. This response let me know that there were some things that the brethren did not understand about forgiveness. I decided then to write this book.

My Mission

This book has been through a five-year process of study and practical application. It has been refined with each step. Studying and teaching about forgiveness has also refined me and given me greater peace.

This book doesn't have all the answers. You may disagree with some of it. But if this book inspires you to study God's Word more or creates a greater love for our Father or motivates you to forgive more and doubt less, then it has been a success.

The focus here is not so much on forgiveness as it is on the nature of God. Many congregations through the years have devoted a considerable amount of time to discussing church organization, proper worship and the plan of salvation. These are important items to study, but we need also to make sure we discuss the nature of God and see how the church, worship, and the plan of salvation fit into the grand scheme of His providential work to save us from our sins. Many lack confidence in salvation while others may have unfounded faith in their salvation because they do not know enough about God and the nature of forgiveness. We see parts of the puzzle but we do not see how it all fits together. Like the scene on the cover of a puzzle box, this book seeks to reveal God's master plan and how the pieces can come together to form a beautiful picture.

When I think of forgiveness, I think of my wife and children. Preaching the gospel is one of the greatest honors and privileges I know of. It is a life filled with rich blessings. It is also a life that can be overwhelming at times. The challenge for me is to leave my worries outside the door of my house. There are times when I bring my frustrations home with me. My family loves me anyway. Every time I have asked my girls to forgive me, they have. They are still excited when I come home. To come home and see their faces pressed against the glass in anticipation, or to see their arms outstretched for a hug, is a precious gift I could never deserve. They are my window into the heart of God. They are my living illustration of what kindness and forgiveness look and feel like.

That is what this book is all about. We will explore forgiveness sought, shown, seized and seen. In other words, we will see why we need forgiveness; we will stand in awe of what God has done to make forgiveness possible; we will explore the means by which we accept forgiveness; and then we will consider how forgiveness is to be seen as it is lived out in the life of the Christian. May our journey along this path help you to find peace.

I hope in some small way this book will be a window into the heart of God for you. I pray that it will open your eyes and awaken your senses to what our gracious God offers us. If we can but get a glimpse into God's heart, then we can see who we are and who we can become. The goal of this book is not just to impart information. It seeks to change our hearts and hands, attitudes and actions into the likeness of Christ. Its mission is to help us find "the peace that passes understanding."

Section 1:
Forgiveness Sought

Chapter 1

The Path
to Peace

P eace. At his second inaugural address in March of 1865, Abraham
Lincoln stated:

> With malice toward none; with charity toward all; with firm-
> ness in the right, as God gives us to see the right, let us strive
> on to finish the work we are in; to bind up the nation's
> wounds; to care for him who shall have borne the battle, and
> for his widow, and his orphan – to do all which may achieve
> and cherish a just, and a lasting peace, among ourselves,
> and with all nations.[1]

Our nation and world have found Lincoln's dream of peace difficult
to realize. Scholars and historians from Norway, England, Egypt,
Germany and India have worked together to collect some sobering information. Since 3600 B.C., the world has experienced only 292 years
of peace! There have been well over 14,000 wars in which 3.64 billion
people have been killed. So much property has been destroyed that
its value could pay for a belt of pure gold that circled the world 97.2
miles wide and 33 feet thick.[2] Even now, war dots the landscape.
American soldiers are stationed all over the world trying desperately
to keep peace. Yet, the struggle hits closer to home as well. On June
12, 1999, I stood on a small hill and looked down on the boarded up

windows of Columbine High School and thought of the children who
died there. And none of us will ever forget the events of Sept. 11, 2001.
Peace? No!

The bloodshed can also be seen in the Lord's church. The cannons
rumble from pen and pulpit, car and conference table. Gone are doc-
trine, mercy, love and forgiveness, the ancient guardians of peace. In
their place we find a flood of "isms," a basic mistrust of each other and
a growing disrespect for the Word of God. Brethren refuse to talk to
each other. Feuds are carried on for years until no one really knows
why they are fighting anymore. Congregation after congregation di-
vides. Others stay together but are in constant turmoil. Peace? No way!

Worry overwhelms us, as well. Parents worry about the safety of their
children. Children worry about everything from peer pressure to living up to their parents' expectations. We worry about the future of
the church. We worry about schools, jobs, bills, deadlines and the list
goes on. We live with knots in our stomachs and can only imagine a
night of sound sleep. We face each day dreading what lies ahead and
wishing life was over. Yet we fear what lies beyond life more than we
fear life itself. We wonder, "Have I done enough?" or "Am I saved?"
We miss the joy of life and dread the uncertainty of death. Peace?
Not a chance!

Herbert Hoover stated, "Peace is not made at the council tables, or
by treaties, but in the hearts of men."[3] This statement is only partially
true. True peace is found when the hearts of human beings are shaped
by the heart of God. We catch a glimpse of the heart of God on the cross
of Calvary: "Father, forgive them" (Luke 23:34). The heart of God
teaches us that the path to peace is paved with forgiveness.

Old Testament Noun for Forgiveness

We will begin our study by looking at the noun used for "forgiveness" in the Old Testament. The first term is *celiychah* (se-lee-**kaw**).[4]
It is translated as "forgiveness" or "pardon," and it is used three times
in the Old Testament (Psalm 130:4; Daniel 9:9; Nehemiah 9:17).[5] In
these three instances, it is presented as an attribute of God and is associated with mercy. Note Nehemiah's use of the term: "But You are
God, Ready to pardon [*celiychah*], Gracious and merciful, Slow to

anger, Abundant in kindness, And did not forsake them" (9:17b).
Nehemiah reveals that forgiveness is treating with mercy one who
deserves anger. Interestingly, the Bible rarely uses the noun form of
forgiveness, in stark contrast to the usage of the verb form of "to forgive." For example, the verb *calach* alone is found 46 times.[6] Seemingly,
the biblical writers put more emphasis on the act of forgiving than on
the concept itself.

Old Testament Verbs for Forgiveness

The first Old Testament verb for "forgive" is *calach* (saw-**lakh**). It
is translated as "forgive, pardon, spare."[7] As we have noted, this term
is found 46 times in the Old Testament and 20 times in the Pentateuch
(the first five books). *Calach* always has God as its subject and is found
most often in the books of Leviticus and Numbers.[8] W.E. Vine notes
that although other terms may be translated "to forgive," *calach* is
the only Old Testament verb with this as its primary meaning.[9] Moses
used this word in Exodus 34:9, "Then he said, 'If now I have found
grace in Your sight, O Lord, let my Lord, I pray, go among us, even
though we are a stiff-necked people; and pardon [*calach*] our iniquity and our sin, and take us as Your inheritance.' " Moses was asking
God to spare the Israelites. He was asking God not to treat them in the
way that they deserved. Notice also the relationship between "go among
us" and "pardon our iniquity." Sin damages the relationship between
God and man. Forgiveness restores that relationship.

The next term for "forgive" in the Old Testament is *nasa'* (naw-**saw**).[10]
Its basic meaning is "to lift, to bear up, to carry, to take."[11] It can include the bearing of punishment, shame and the like.[12] In certain set-
tings, it can be translated "to forgive, pardon"; it is used as such approximately 15 times. It is "an alleviation of the burden of guilt, the
removal of the divisive barrier, and the bridging of the separation."[13]
The term was used to explain that sinners must bear the weight of their
sins (Leviticus 19:8). *Nasa'* was also used in the sense that the priests
bore the sins of the people (Numbers 18:23). They had the responsibility of making atonement for the people in the tabernacle. Ultimately,
however, only God could bear sin, "The Lord is longsuffering and abundant in mercy, forgiving [*nasa'*] iniquity and transgression" (Numbers

14:18). Although *nasa'* is not used, Isaiah 53:6 foresees a day when the suffering servant, Jesus Christ, would bear the weight of our sins. Although the words *calach* and *kaphar* are used only in reference to the forgiveness of God, *nasa'* is used for both divine and human forgiveness (Genesis 50:17).[14]

Another key verb is *kaphar* (kaw-**far**). This term is often found hand-in-hand with *calach*. They are joined 12 times in Leviticus and Numbers (Leviticus 4:20, 26, 31, 35).[15] The verb *kaphar* means "to cover, to purge, to make an atonement, to make reconciliation, to cover over with pitch."[16] Atonement (*kaphar*) makes pardon (*calach*) possible. We will discuss the concept of atonement further in a later chapter.[17]

Several other important terms are found in Psalm 51. This chapter has been called, "the liturgy of the broken heart."[18] David prayed, "Have mercy upon me, O God, According to Your lovingkindness; According to the multitude of Your tender mercies, *Blot out* my transgressions. *Wash me* thoroughly from my iniquity, And *cleanse* me from my sin. ... *Purge me* with hyssop, and I shall be clean; *Wash me*, and I shall be whiter than snow. ... *Hide Your face* from my sins, And *blot out* all my iniquities" (51:1-2, 7, 9; emphasis mine).[19]

"Blot out" in Psalm 51:1 is the word *machah* (maw-**khaw**). It literally means "to stroke or rub" and by implication "to erase."[20] Keil and Delitzsch note that "sins are conceived of as a cumulative debt ... written down ... against the time of the payment by punishment."[21] This reading stresses that sin deserves punishment. The picture in Psalm 51 is of a judgment scene in which the crimes of the defendant are read before the judge. The judge then pronounces the sentence. David sought to have the list of his sins erased so that he would not have to face the righteous wrath of the judge. Moses and God used this term in Exodus 32:32-33. Moses asked God to forgive (*nasa'*) the Israelites of the sin of the golden calf or else to blot (*machah*) his name out of God's book.[22] Moses was putting himself on the line for the people. When we compare this text with Psalm 51, we get a powerful picture. Either we will have the lists of our sins erased or our names will be erased from the list of the saved.

In connection with the "blotting out" of sin, David requested that God, "Hide Your face from my sins" (Psalm 51:9). "Hide" comes from the word *cathar* (saw-**thar**).[23] Sin is seen as an offense against God. It is against His very nature. Isaiah said, "And your sins have hidden His face from you, So that He will not hear" (Isaiah 59:2b). God's nature is repulsed by sin. It causes Him to turn His face from us. David asked God to turn His face from his sin and not from David himself.

"Wash" (Psalm 51:2) is the term *kabac* (kaw-**bas**). It means "to trample; hence, to wash (properly, by stamping with the feet)."[24] This is a deeper cleaning than merely rinsing with water (*rachats* in Hebrew). "Iniquity is conceived of as deeply ingrained dirt."[25] David also used the term *taher*, (taw-**hare**, "cleanse me") in verse 2. This is the common term for "make clean." It can refer to being made clean physically, ceremonially, or morally.[26] *Taher* was used 37 times in Leviticus 11–15 in connection with the ritual purity laws.[27] These laws taught the children of Israel that uncleanness affects their relationship with God. Israelites could not approach the tabernacle in an unclean state. Isaiah said, "But your iniquities have separated you from your God" (Isaiah 59:2a). David understood this separation as well, which is why he requested, "Do not cast me away from Your presence, And do not take Your Holy Spirit from me" (Psalm 51:11). These two terms, *kabac* and *taher*, reveal a common theme in the Old Testament: sin defiles and makes one unclean.

David emphasized that sin was "against" God in Psalm 51:4. This psalm, written in the aftermath of David's sin with Bathsheba, shows that David knew he had ultimately sinned against God. He had violated God's will and thus had incurred guilt and the accompanying punishment. Only God could purify and restore the broken relationship. God's forgiveness was contingent upon David's willingness to acknowledge his sins (v. 3).

Conclusion

Our overview of the forgiveness terms in the Old Testaments brings out several key concepts. We have seen that sin defiles, deserves punishment and damages the relationship between God and man. Sin is truly a deadly business. One writer has said that anyone "who equates sin with bad habits is comparable to a physician who encourages a cancer patient in the self-deception that a probable tumor is just 'a little bump' that will go away by itself." [28]

Our study has revealed that because God is the one wronged, God must do the forgiving. We learned that forgiveness is the restoring of a relationship by treating with kindness someone who deserves anger. We also observed that there must be atonement for sin before forgiveness can take place. Forgiveness is the removal of the barriers that separate God and human beings. [29]

John Greenleaf Whittier wrote, "Drop thy still dews of quietness, Till all our strivings cease; Take from our souls the strain and stress, And let our ordered lives confess, The beauty of thy peace." [30] Whittier correctly understood that true peace lies with God. Our focus on biblical terms has reminded us that sin is a barrier to that peace. Let's explore how this problem started.

Discussion Questions

1. What are the roadblocks to peace in your life?

2. What do you hope to learn about forgiveness from this book?

3. What are three insights into the definition forgiveness you have gained from this chapter?

Looking Ahead

Do you think that the temptations Eve faced in the garden are different from the types of temptations we face today?

Chapter 2

"This Snake Is Gorgeous"

More than 3,000 kinds of snakes exist in the world. They come in many shapes and sizes. The longest snake ever measured was a Reticulated Python measuring more than 32 feet. The heaviest snake ever weighed was a 600-pound anaconda. The oldest snake on record was 40 years old (in a zoo). The shortest snake is the thread snake which may be as little as 4 inches when full grown. Snakes range in color from the bright green of the eastern green mamba to the almost colorless skin of the thread snake.[1] Have you ever watched a nature show that talked about dangerous snakes? I think of a show called *The Crocodile Hunter* and its host, Steve Irwin. Irwin has often been seen picking up a deadly cobra and saying, "This snake is gorgeous." They may be gorgeous to some, but they can also be deadly.

As dangerous as these snakes are, there is an ancient serpent that is even more dangerous. It is the serpent mentioned in Genesis 3. Many a camper has worried that a snake will crawl into his sleeping bag to keep warm. Yet, we often freely allow the devil to have access to our lives. His venom poisons our relationship with God.

Perfection of God's Creations

Why did God make the world? Did He need something? No. We cannot give God anything He does not already have (cf. Psalm 144:3-4;

Acts 17:25). Was He lonely? No. He had companionship and love
before the creation. Jesus said of the Father, "You loved Me before the
foundation of the world" (John 17:24b). God was not alone or incomplete. Creation was a choice of His will, unmotivated by any need
on His part. But the Bible does reveal one attribute of God that motivates His actions throughout history: "God so loved the World" (John
3:16). First John 4:8 says, "God is love." Love is a part of His nature.
Does love share or take? Does it build or destroy? God created the world
because of His loving nature. He created because love seeks to express
itself by giving, helping and creating.

You have probably heard the saying, "It isn't a perfect world." That is
true now, but it was not always so. God's love motivated Him to create
a perfect world. Six times in Genesis 1 God looked at what He had created and called it "good." The seventh time He called it "very good"
(v. 31). The only time God said it was "not good" was in 2:18 when He
saw the loneliness of Adam. He then fixed that problem by creating Eve.
It was a perfect world in the sense that it was not flawed. Adam and Eve
lived in a beautiful garden paradise with no death, thorns or thistles. There
wasn't even rain to cancel the Eden Softball Tournament. It was perfect!

Why emphasize the flawless nature of creation? Because we often
blame God for the pain, suffering, sorrow and death in the world. None
of these things were present when God made the world. What *was* present, however, was choice. God did not create robots or slaves. He created human beings with the freedom to choose to love Him or not to love
Him. True love involves risk. Parents who create a child as an expres-
sion of their love take risks. The child may grow sick or even die. The
child may grow up and reject the love and teaching of the parents. God
chose, in His sovereign will, to take similar risks when He created us.
He wanted humanity's love for Him to be a free choice, not something
they were forced to do. In order to have freedom of choice, there must
be different options. That is why the possibility of evil was allowed.

God warned man about the dangers of this evil by saying, "[B]ut
of the tree of the knowledge of good and evil you shall not eat" (Genesis
2:17). We must remember that God made a flawless world and only
presented the possibility of evil because He wanted to have a loving
relationship with us. Human beings chose evil over that relationship.

Purpose for Man

Although the world God created was perfect in the sense that it was not flawed, it was not complete. God had more in store for the creation. We have considered why God created and found the answer to be love. Now we need to consider the "what" of creation. What did God have in mind for His creation? What was our purpose to be?

We have already noted that we were created to be in a relationship with God, but there's more. We were also created to be His representatives. God made us in His image (Genesis 1:26-28). What does that mean? The word "image" is the Hebrew term *tselem* (**tseh**-lem). It is found 16 times in the Old Testament and basically means "a representation" or "a likeness." It is used most often when speaking of idols, but it is used five times to refer to the fact that we are made in the image of God.[2] Some believe that "image" refers to man's ability to reason. Others point to the fact that we have an eternal soul. Still others point to our unique ability to have a relationship with God. Each of these descriptions has validity, but they still do not fully define what "image" means.

Tselem was used to describe images that kings of the ancient Near East often left of themselves in locations throughout their empire where they could not be present. Stanley Grenz notes, "Such images served to represent their majesty and power."[3] Could it be that God's "image" not only speaks of something in our nature but also points us to our purpose? Notice the text of Genesis 1:26: "Let Us make man in Our image, according to Our likeness; let them have dominion over … all the earth." God also said, "Be fruitful and multiply; fill the earth and subdue it" (v. 28). God created the world so that it might be filled with people with whom He could have a relationship. He never intended for creation to end in the garden. He called on humanity to go on creating new life through procreation. He created Adam and Eve to fulfill His purposes. They were created as His representatives to rule over and fill the earth. We were created not only for a relationship with God but also to represent Him and carry out His will on the earth. We must recognize that if we are to represent or "image" God accurately in the world we must look like Him. We must live as He would live on the earth and love as He loves His creation.

Pied Piper

Robert Browning's poem, "The Pied Piper of Hamelin," tells of Hamelin Town, a city infested with rats. A young man happens along and says he will rid the town of the vermin for a price. The mayor and town leaders agree to the amount, and the young man then begins to play his pipe. All the rats follow him out of town and into the river where they drown. When the mayor reneges on the promised price, the young man plays his pipe again, and all the children follow him out of town, never to be seen again. Genesis 3 tells of another piper who seeks to lead God's children away from relationship and representation to drown them in a river of sin.

Jacob blessed his 12 sons from his deathbed in Genesis 49. When Jacob blessed Dan he said, "Dan shall be a serpent by the way, A viper by the path, That bites the horse's heels So that its rider shall fall backward" (v. 17). Jacob was probably referring to the horned adder, a poisonous snake and a danger to travelers (both horse and man). It was sand-colored and hid in the sand along the path to strike an unaware traveler.[4] The deceptive nature of this serpent is consistent with the description of the serpent in Genesis 3:1, "Now the serpent was more cunning than any beast of the field which the Lord God had made."

Satan took the form of a serpent because the Bible describes Satan as deceptive and treacherous (John 8:44; 2 Corinthians 11:14; Ephesians 6:11; 1 Timothy 3:7; Revelation 12:9; 20:2). It is important for us to understand this fact about the devil. He does not fight fairly. He does not come out with a big sign that says, "HEY, I'M THE DEVIL. WATCH OUT!" He lies and cheats and makes evil look good. He is the master of deception. He knows where your weak spots are, and he tries to exploit them. But God always provides a way of escape (1 Corinthians 10:13). We just need to look for it!

Pattern of Attack

Different snakes have different patterns to aid in hiding or in capturing their prey. The southern copperhead has a bright yellow tail. It wiggles its tail in front of a frog to get its attention while the front end of the snake moves to striking position. Satan has his own pattern of attack as well. He caught Eve while she was alone. Although we may be led into sin by the influence of the crowd, often we are alone when we face our greatest temptations. Satan also began his attack on Eve by creating doubt in her mind: "Has God indeed said, 'You shall not eat of every tree of the garden'?"(Genesis 3:1b). He was saying, "You have got to be kidding. Did God really say you couldn't eat from all the trees in the garden?" He was planting doubt in her mind about God's goodness.

Eve responded by saying that God restricted them from eating from only one tree, and the penalty for eating from that tree was death (Genesis 3:3). Having already planted doubt in her mind, Satan responded with an outright lie: "You will not surely die" (v. 4). Satan attacked God directly. He still works that way. He says, "God isn't real" or "God doesn't care about you" or "If God is real, why do bad things happen?" Jesus called Satan the father of lies (John 8:44). He doesn't tell you the truth. He doesn't say, "Alcohol kills people and destroys lives." He says instead, "If you want to have fun, be cool and date the best looking girls, then you need to drink." Don't believe his lies! Don't believe the false propaganda his agents spread.

Satan attacked Eve's weaknesses. He attacked her pleasure: "[T]he tree was good for food"; her perception: "[I]t was pleasant to the eyes"; and her pride: "[D]esirable to make one wise." Satan used the same pattern when tempting Jesus (Matthew 4:1-11; Luke 4:1-13). He said, "[C]ommand this stone to become bread" (Luke 4:3; lust of the flesh). He offered Jesus the kingdoms of the earth (lust of the eyes). Satan challenged Him to throw Himself from the pinnacle of the Temple because God would catch Him (pride of life).

The apostle John said, "Do not love the world or the things in the world. If anyone loves the world, the love of the Father is not in him. For all that is in the world – the lust of the flesh, the lust of the eyes, and the pride of life – is not of the Father but is of the world" (1 John 2:15-17). This is a consistent pattern that still works today. Satan tells us, "It will be fun" (pleasure/lust of the flesh), "Doesn't she look good" (perception/lust of the eyes), or "Everyone will like you" (pride of life). Eve had been created in God's image as His representative. She chose to represent herself, and Adam followed her lead. She forgot her purpose.

Satan attacked the very foundation of society – the home. Marriage and family were to be the cure for loneliness (Genesis 2:18-24) and function as a conduit for the spreading of the laws of God throughout the human race (Deuteronomy 6:6-9). Satan was aware of this plan and consequently launched his attacks upon the family unit. In Genesis 3, he turned husband and wife against each other and their God. In Genesis 4, he turned brother against brother. Society then spiraled downward until God found a righteous family with whom He could begin anew (Noah). When you look at God's laws relative to the family, you find that God speaks with strong language (Exodus 20:12, 14; Deuteronomy 22:22; Matthew 19:1-10; Romans 1:30-31). He is protecting the very foundation of society. We must guard our families at all costs against the Serpent's attacks.

Price for Disobedience

Just as the southern copperhead with the yellow tail lulls the frog into dropping its defenses, so Satan lulled Eve into dropping hers. Then he struck with a deadly blow, and his fangs sank deep. In the process, Satan literally turned creation upside down. The order of authority in creation had been God, man, woman and creatures (Genesis 2). The fall of man began with a creature tempting woman, who tempted man, out of a desire to be like God. This was the opposite of what God had planned. As Satan's venom pulsed through their veins, Adam and Eve realized that sin came at a price. Their pain was emotional (shame for their nakedness), physical (childbirth/tilling the ground) and spiritual (damaging their relationship with God). Before the fall, Eve was able to have children, and Adam could find food. After the fall, these tasks were more difficult – their sin made everything more difficult.

It is the same for us. When we choose to disobey God, pain inevitably follows. It may not come immediately, but it comes. We suffer emotionally as we struggle with the guilt of what we have done. We are embarrassed to talk about it. We are afraid others will find out. We suffer physically as well. We can't sleep at night, and our stomachs are in knots. The most serious pain, however, is spiritual. Our sin separates us from the God who loves us and longs to save us (Isaiah 59:1-2; Romans 6:23; James 1:13-15). Adam and Eve lost paradise over a piece of fruit. What about us?

Conclusion

David and Vera Gray own a Christmas tree farm in Hatley, Miss. David is an elder of the Christian Chapel congregation where I once served as pulpit minister. One day while cleaning up around the farm, he reached over a log and was bitten on the hand by a large copperhead. He still bears the scars to this day.

Every human being has been bitten by Satan (Romans 3:23). Do you bear the scars of sin? If the devil's venom is coursing through your veins, then you better get some anti-venom soon, before it is too late. The garden tells us why we must seek forgiveness; the altar will show us how God has shown forgiveness. Our next lesson will begin to explore the steps God has taken to save us and repair the broken relationship.

Discussion Questions

1. How do you feel about the presence of evil in the world?

2. What are some ways the devil tricks us today?

3. Have your life experiences shown you that there are physical, spiritual and emotional consequences of sin?

Looking Ahead

What is the theme of the Bible?

Section 2:
Forgiveness Shown

Chapter 3

The Thread

Have you ever seen a pearl necklace? If so, you will notice that the beautiful pearls are held together by some kind of thread or string. Without this thread, the pearls would fall to the floor and become lost. Each book of the Bible is a beautiful pearl, a revelation from God that tells us something of His will for humanity. Something will be lost if we do not see the thread that runs through each document.

We noted at the beginning of the last lesson that love is what motivated God to create and to act in human history. As Israel stood on the threshold of the Promised Land, Moses declared to the people, "And because He loved your fathers, therefore He chose their descendants after them; and He brought you out of Egypt with His Presence, with His mighty power" (Deuteronomy 4:37). The queen of Sheba told Solomon, "Because your God has loved Israel, ... He made you king over them" (2 Chronicles 9:8).

Thomas Raitt surveyed the more than 200 forgiveness passages in the Old Testament and found 20 different reasons God forgives humanity.[1] He found that the most common reason was love,[2] especially as expressed by the Hebrew word *chesed*, meaning "goodness, kindness, faithfulness."[3] John summed it up best when he stated, "We love Him because He first loved us" (1 John 4:19). The motivation for the existence of the world is love. With love comes a relationship.

Remember Moses' words, "[B]ecause He loved your fathers, … He brought you out of Egypt with His Presence" (Deuteronomy 4:37). Scripture reveals God's efforts to be present among humanity. This chapter will explore God's relationship with His people throughout the Old Testament story.

The Creation

God walked in the garden with Adam and Eve, but that relationship changed when sin entered the picture. "And they heard the sound of the Lord God walking in the garden in the cool of the day, and Adam and his wife hid themselves from the presence of the Lord God" (Genesis 3:8). Sin resulted in humanity's expulsion from the garden "lest he put out his hand and take also of the tree of life, and eat, and live forever" (v. 22). Removal from the tree of life was actually an act of grace – it prevented humanity from living forever in a sinful state, in a fallen world, and away from the presence of God. Even in this time of sorrow, a ray of hope was revealed as God prophesied that the seed of woman (Jesus Christ) would fatally wound the serpent (v. 15).

The story of the fall does not end here. Humanity plummeted further downward from the fall until "the Lord was sorry that He had made man on the earth" (Genesis 6:6). God corrected creation by cleansing it with the flood. He found a new representative with whom He could have a relationship. Still the downward spiral of sin continued – humanity hit rock bottom in Genesis 11 at the tower of Babel. Notice the contrast between chapters 1 and 11:

Genesis 1	Genesis 11
v. 26 "Then God said, 'Let Us make man in Our image, according to Our likeness; let them have dominion over the fish of the sea.' " v. 28 "Then God blessed them, and God said to them, 'Be fruitful and multiply; fill the earth and subdue it.' "	v. 4 "And they said, 'Come, let us build ourselves a city, and a tower whose top is in the heavens; let us make a name for ourselves, lest we be scattered abroad over the face of the whole earth.' "

Humans were created to represent God; they were to make a name for Him and carry out His will in the earth. They chose to do the opposite. This resulted in broken relationships (i.e., confusing the languages). Failure to represent God results in broken relationships with both God and people. What about us? Have we chosen to represent ourselves instead of God? The Bible is the story of God's efforts to restore the broken relationship and to seek people who will represent Him in the world.

The Covenant

As we have already noted, in the midst of humanity's downward spiral God sent a flood to "destroy man" (Genesis 6:7). However, God found one man, Noah, with whom He could have a relationship and with whom He could start anew. God later established a lasting relationship with one of Noah's descendants, a man named Abram (12:1-4). God promised Abram a great nation and a great land, but the most important promise He made was to bless all nations of the earth through him. God told Abram, "I will bless you … And you shall be a blessing" (v. 2). Here we learn a valuable lesson. God does not bless us for our benefit alone. He blesses us that we might bless others.

Abram became God's special representative. Through Abram's seed, God restored the relationship with humanity that had been broken by sin. God maintained a relationship with Abram's descendants Isaac, Jacob and Joseph. Even when the children of Israel found themselves slaves in Egypt, God stepped forward as their redeemer. He delivered them from their enemies. He then established a covenant relationship with them at Mount Sinai (Exodus 19:5). The Ten Commandments describe how people are to act if they are in a relationship with a holy God, like the vows spoken at a wedding ceremony. The first four commandments elaborate on our relationship with God and the greatest command, "Love the Lord your God" (Deuteronomy 6:5; Matthew 22:37). The last six commandments elaborate on the second great commandment, "Love your neighbor" (Leviticus 19:18; Matthew 22:39). The remaining commands in the Old Testament are an elaboration on the original 10. They are basically "case laws" telling us how to apply the Ten Commandments to given situations.

God walked with the Israelites because they were in a covenant relationship with Him. God's presence was seen in the cloud that guided them. God's presence was what separated them from the other nations. And their relationship with God was also to be a light to the nations. God told them they were to "be to Me a kingdom of priests and a holy nation" (Exodus 19:6). They were not merely chosen for their benefit alone. Like Abram, they were blessed to be a blessing. They were to be priests, or mediators, between God and the rest of humanity. Despite this tremendous blessing and opportunity, Israel rebelled against God even as He was on the mountain giving Moses the vows for their marriage covenant.

The Israelites chose a relationship with a lifeless idol over the living God. In the aftermath of the golden calf, they realized once again that God is a God of justice who punishes sin. We see both God's anger and His mercy in the incredible offer He made to Moses in Exodus 33. God told Israel to go to the land He had promised to give them. He said that He would send His angel before them and drive out their enemies. He kept His word to Abraham, Isaac and Jacob. But, He said, "I will not go up in your midst, lest I consume you on the way, for you are a stiff-necked people" (v. 3). The people mourned this terrible news. They did not want the promised land if God was not there with them. The world's riches are worthless if we have no relationship with God.

Moses set up his tent "outside the camp, far from the camp, and called it the tabernacle of meeting" (Exodus 33:7). The placement of the tent outside the camp was symbolic of the broken relationship between God and Israel. A powerful picture is portrayed in Exodus 33:8-11. When Moses went to meet with God in the tabernacle, the people stood at the doors of their tents and watched. They longed to have their relationship with God restored. These were no doubt tense moments. Would God speak with Moses? Would God go with them? When the cloud came down in front of the tent, the people worshiped. There was hope!

On behalf of the people, Moses interceded and proclaimed, "If Your Presence does not go with us, do not bring us up from here" (Exodus 33:15). God honored Moses' request and even gave him a glimpse of His glory (vv. 17-23). Later a man greater than Moses would aid all humanity in their relationship with God (cf. Hebrews 3:3ff).

The two key Old Testament verbs for forgiveness, *calach* and *nasa'*, are found in connection with the sin of the golden calf. The Bible had little to say directly about forgiveness before that event, which stresses how pivotal the golden calf incident was in the history of God's people. *Nasa'* (bear/forgive) was used in Exodus 32:32. Here Moses put himself on the line for the people and asked God to forgive the people or strike his name from God's book. *Nasa'* was also used by God in Exodus 34:7 to describe Himself as He gave the commandments a second time, emphasizing that God forgave them and was willing to stay in a covenant relationship with them. *Calach* (pardon) was used by Moses in Exodus 34:9 as he asked God to pardon their iniquity and "go among" them.[4] These terms show that forgiveness and God's presence are intimately united.

The Communion

Despite their sins, God still sought communion and fellowship with the Israelites. No more graphic example of this desire exists than the tabernacle. God commanded the Israelites to construct a special tent to symbolize His presence among them (Exodus 25ff). Exodus 40:34ff portrays God's presence filling the tabernacle. God cannot be limited to a building made with human hands (cf. Acts 17:24-25), but there was a sense in which He was present in the Most Holy Place of the tabernacle. As they looked to the tabernacle and the cloud, the Israelites were reminded that God was among them. They were in communion with the Creator of the universe. Their every move was guided by the Lord. They traveled only when the cloud moved. The tabernacle being placed in the middle of the camp stands in stark contrast to Exodus 33:7 when the tent was "far from the camp."

The people learned that there were repercussions to having God in their midst. The book of Leviticus details what is necessary for God to dwell among sinful people. The Israelites also came to understand the concept of atonement. The verb *kaphar* (to make atonement) is found 49 times in Leviticus (102 occurrences in the entire Old Testament).[5] Atonement made forgiveness possible. The purpose of the sacrificial system and atonement was re-establishing the relationship between human beings and God.[6]

Calach (pardon/forgive) is found 10 times in Leviticus 4-6 to describe what happened in connection with the sin and guilt offerings.[7] The tabernacle not only showed the people that God was among them but also the distance that existed between God and the people. The layout of the Israelite camp in Numbers confirms this. God was present in the Most Holy Place. Beyond this were the Holy Place, the courtyard, the encampment of the Levites, the camp of Israel, the area of uncleanness and the wilderness, respectively. There were degrees of access to God, but He was still in their midst, and that was a precious blessing.

The ongoing story of Israel shows a pattern of rejection in their relationship with the Father. They doubted the strength of their God even as they stood on the doorstep of the Promised Land. Fear caused them to listen to the negative report of the 10 spies instead of the faithful report of the two. The entire generation of people who had been freed from Egypt, except Caleb and Joshua, forfeited the "land flowing with milk and honey" (cf. Numbers 13-14). Once again Moses interceded on their behalf. He pleaded, " 'The Lord is longsuffering and abundant in mercy, forgiving [*nasa'*] iniquity and transgression; but He by no means clears the guilty, visiting the iniquity of the fathers on the children to the third and fourth generation.' Pardon [*calach*] the iniquity of this people, I pray, according to the greatness of Your mercy, just as You have forgiven [*nasa'*] this people, from Egypt even until now" (Numbers 14:18-19). God responded, "I have pardoned [*calach*], according to your word" (v. 20). In Numbers 15:25-31, we learn that God forgives (*calach*) inadvertent sin, but He does not forgive presumptuous sin. Inadvertent or unintentional sin can include sin that one knew was wrong; whereas presumptuous sin might be defined as highhanded sin in which one willfully and openly defies God. It is an attitude of shaking one's fist in the face of God.

The aftermath of the spies' negative report revealed a God who punishes sin but also keeps His promises and renews His covenant. He gave a new generation possession of the land of Canaan. Later, Solomon built the temple as a permanent sanctuary for the Lord. God no longer dwelt in a tent. This change was significant because the temple symbolized that God's presence was with them, that they were no longer nomads, and that they were firmly settled in the land God had promised them.

The temple also stresses to us that forgiveness and God's presence are intimately joined. In 1 Kings 8:28ff and 2 Chronicles 6:19, Solomon asked the Lord to forgive (*calach*) those who confess, repent and pray from or toward the temple in which God dwells. God told Solomon that He would honor his request: "[I]f my people who are called by My name will humble themselves, and pray and seek My face, and turn from their wicked ways, then I will hear from heaven, and will forgive [*calach*] their sin and heal their land" (2 Chronicles 7:14).[8]

The Call

Despite an incredible promise from God, the children of Israel continually rejected Him. He then sent His prophets to call them back into communion with Him, but the Israelites did not listen. God finally turned them over to their enemies, and they were taken away into exile by the Assyrians and Babylonians. Ezekiel 10 describes God's presence moving from the temple and out through the gate on the eastern side of Jerusalem.

Forgiveness is a recurring theme in the writings of the prophets.[9] One can divide this usage into four categories. The first usage is negative in nature. It refers to what God will not forgive and the judgment coming upon the nation for rejecting God (Isaiah 2:9; Jeremiah 5:7; Lamentations 3:42). Forty of the more than 200 forgiveness passages in the Old Testament speak of God deciding not to forgive.[10]

The second category consists of calls from God or the prophets for the people to repent so they might avoid God's judgment (Isaiah 55:6-7; Jeremiah 5:1; 36:1-3). Jeremiah uses the word "repent" 111 times.[11] The third usage involves pleas from the prophets for God to forgive the people (Daniel 9:19; Amos 7:1-3).

The final and most prominent usage of the forgiveness terms among the prophets foresees a day when God will once again forgive His people (Isaiah 33:21-24; Jeremiah 31:31-34; 33:7-8; 50:18-20; Micah 7:18-20). Repentance, humility and obedience were prerequisites of this forgiveness. The final category stresses that God would not forsake His promise. He would continue to seek a relationship. Although sin would hinder man's relationship with God, it could never stop God's will from being carried out.

The prophets envisioned a day when God would establish a new covenant with a remnant of Israel. Two passages are significant in this regard. The first is Jeremiah 31:31-34 where Jeremiah spoke of a new covenant God would establish with Israel and Judah. In this covenant there is a bond between relationship and forgiveness. Jeremiah said that in the new covenant, "[T]hey all shall know Me, from the least of them to the greatest of them, says the Lord. For I will forgive [*calach*] their iniquity, and their sin I will remember no more" (v. 34). Another powerful passage is Micah 7:18-20,

> Who is a God like You, Pardoning [*nasa'*] iniquity And passing over the transgression of the remnant of His heritage? He does not retain His anger forever, because He delights in mercy. He will again have compassion on us, And will subdue our iniquities. You will cast all our sins Into the depths of the sea. You will give truth to Jacob And mercy to Abraham, Which You have sworn to our fathers From days of old.

The language Micah used was from Exodus 15:11 and 34:6-7. He was saying that the God who delivered Israel from Egypt and forgave her at Mount Sinai would still forgive.[12] God was still calling out to His people.

Beginning in Ezekiel 40, the new temple is described. Ezekiel 43:4-5 depicts the Spirit of the Lord returning to the temple. The prophets foresaw a day when the relationship would be renewed and God would once again be present with His people. The New Testament tells us that "the Word" became flesh and "dwelt/tabernacled" among us (John 1:14). Through Jesus Christ, God came to live in the midst of humanity, and we came to know Him as never before (cf. Jeremiah 31:34).

Jesus came as God's representative to repair the relationship once again and to call out a people who would represent God in the world. The church (1 Corinthians 3:16-17) and the Christian (6:19-20) have become the temple in which God's Spirit dwells. We are to be His representatives. The writer of Hebrews ties Christ's covenant back to the prophecy of Jeremiah 31 (cf. Hebrews 8). Finally, the book of Revelation describes a heavenly scene which stands in stark contrast to that of Leviticus when only the high priest could enter the most holy place of the tabernacle. In Revelation we see the saved dwelling in the very presence of God (Revelation 21:21-27). The sin that had previously defiled the tabernacle and destroyed the relationship between God and man will not be present in the heavenly Jerusalem (Revelation 21:27). God's people will live in the Most Holy Place for eternity.

Conclusion

As we journey through the Old Testament, we see a God who is reaching out to His creation. He acts on humanity's behalf so that they might succeed and enjoy His blessings. The people's sins continue to get in the way. Our survey of forgiveness in the Old Testament reminds us of the intimate connection between God's presence (relationship) and God's forgiveness (remission). The story of the Bible is the story of God acting on behalf of humanity to restore their broken relationship. Forgiveness represents the resumption of that relationship. Wayne Jackson summarizes the theme of the Bible as "the redemption of fallen man by means of the mission of Christ, to the ultimate glory of God." [13] Jackson also outlines the Bible as generation (the creation), degeneration (the fall), and regeneration (God's efforts to save), the bulk being about regeneration. "For God so loved the world that He gave His only begotten Son" is the thread that runs through the pearls that make up God's Word (John 3:16).

Dallas Willard tells the story of a pilot practicing high-speed maneuvers in a jet fighter. When the pilot turned the controls to fly upward, she slammed into the ground. She did not realize that she was flying upside down. [14] Genesis 3-11 shows a world that is flying upside down. Humanity had reversed God's original plan for His creation. The story of the Bible is the story of God helping His creation to see that what they think is right side up is in fact upside down. Ed Wharton has noted, "Religion is from two Latin words, *re* meaning 'back,' and *lego* meaning 'to bind.' Thus, religion is God's system of binding sinful man back to God." [15] By focusing on the Day of Atonement, we can see how God acted on behalf of humanity to remove the problem of sin and bind us back to Him.

Discussion Questions

1. Do you agree that love was the reason God made the world?

2. Do you think John 3:16 is a good theme verse for the Bible? Why?

3. How can being aware of the fact that God is seeking a relationship with us affect the way we live and think?

Looking Ahead

Why did Israel offer sacrifices under the Old Law?

Chapter 4

The Day of Atonement: Preparation

I have had the privilege of hearing two former presidents and a former president's wife speak. I find it interesting to watch the Secret Service at these events. They are responsible for protecting the president and his family (among others). The following information is found on the Secret Service website and summarizes how they prepare for the president when he goes to any given area.

> The Secret Service does not discuss methods or means in any detail, however generally speaking, the advance team surveys each site to be visited. From these surveys, the members determine manpower, equipment, hospitals, and evacuation routes for emergencies. Fire, rescue, and other public service personnel in the community are alerted. A command post is established with full communications facilities. The assistance of the military, federal, state, county, and local law enforcement organizations is a vital part of the entire security operation.
>
> Before the protectee's arrival, the lead advance agent coordinates all law enforcement representatives participating in

the visit. Personnel are posted and are alerted to specific problems associated with the visit. Intelligence information is discussed, identification specified, and emergency options outlined. Prior to the arrival of the protectee, checkpoints are established, and access to the secured area is limited.[1]

It is fascinating to consider all that is involved in preparing for a visit by the president of the United States. In light of this, imagine what it is like when the Creator of the universe comes to visit. We learned in our last chapter that God seeks to dwell among His people. He wants a personal relationship with us. We also learned in the book of Leviticus that a holy God cannot dwell with sinful and unclean people. Their sins must be atoned for, and their impurities must be cleansed. What must take place before God can visit and live with human beings?

The next two chapters will focus on the Day of Atonement as presented in Leviticus 16, although the phrase "Day of Atonement" is not actually found in Leviticus 16. It is found in the plural form ("Day of Atonements") in Leviticus 23:27-28 and 25:9. Modern Jews refer to this day as Yom Kippur. Why spend two chapters of our study on this one event? R.K. Harrison helps us to see why by describing Leviticus 16 as "the ceremonial and theological pivot upon which the entire book of Leviticus turns."[2]

The preceding chapters set the stage. Sin and uncleanness, as previously noted, place a barrier between humanity and God. God instituted a sacrificial system (Leviticus 1–7) and revealed His laws on ritual purity (11–15). He also installed a priesthood (8–10) to perform the necessary sacrifices, to distinguish between the holy and profane and the unclean and clean, and to teach God's statutes (10:10-11). Jacob Milgrom states that the ritual purity laws in chapters 11–15 specify "the impurities that can pollute the sanctuary (15:31), for which the purification rite of chapter 16 is mandated."[3] Thus, the discussion in chapter 16 brings together all that precedes it. It also serves as preparation for the teaching on holy living that follows. God's people were motivated to live in the manner described in chapters 17–26 by the fact that their sins had been ransomed and removed on the Day of Atonement.

Gordon Wenham notes that it was inevitable that someone would unwittingly violate the purity laws described in Leviticus 11–15 and pollute the tabernacle where God dwelt.[4] Leviticus tells us that sin defiles and pollutes all that it touches, including the tabernacle of God. Part of the purpose of the Day of Atonement was to cleanse the tabernacle symbolically of the defilement of the people's sins. Its purpose also included the removal of sin by substitutionary sacrifice – an animal is substituted for a person. The Day of Atonement shows us how God dealt with sin. It teaches what was necessary in order to enjoy forgiveness. These principles are then played out in the rest of the history of Israel.

That is why we are spending two chapters discussing the Day of Atonement. This chapter will focus on the past (Leviticus 16:1-2) and the preparation (vv. 3-5). The next chapter will focus on the purification (vv. 6-28) and the placement (vv. 29-34).

The Past (Leviticus 16:1-2)

We begin our study of the Day of Atonement by looking at the connection between the events of chapter 16 and the past. The text begins by saying, "Now the Lord spoke to Moses" (Leviticus 16:1). God did speak directly to Aaron (10:8; Numbers 18:1), but His normal pattern was to speak through Moses, emphasizing the special role of Moses in the Pentateuch. He was the priest's priest.

Leviticus 16:1 also reminds us that the rituals described in the book of Leviticus must not be detached from their historical setting. A narrative string holds the pearls together. Verse 1 ties chapter 16 back to chapter 10 and the deaths of Nadab and Abihu. God sought to keep Aaron from suffering the same fate as his sons. God is not arbitrary in the making of His laws. They are often designed to protect humanity. We must be very careful in how we approach a holy God. Nadab and Abihu approached God improperly. We learned as small children that we are not to touch a hot stove or to stick our hand into a roaring campfire. Likewise, we must be careful in the presence of God. It is not that He does not love us; our nature is simply different from His, just as the nature of fire and human flesh are different.

God told Moses to tell Aaron "not to come at just any time into the Holy Place" (Leviticus 16:2), meaning he was not to enter the Most Holy Place anytime he wanted. Aaron was to enter only at a specific time and under very specific conditions. It is a very dangerous thing to come into the presence of God ("lest he die"). God's presence was "above the mercy seat." Described in Exodus 25:17-22, the mercy seat was a slab of gold 2½ by 1½ cubits that covered the ark. On it were two golden cherubim with outstretched wings that touched one another. The Hebrew noun used in Exodus was *kapporet*, translated "cover." It comes from the verb *kaphar* which means, "to cover, to purge, to make an atonement, to make reconciliation, to cover over with pitch."[5] *Kapporet* is used in the Old Testament only in connection with the ark of the covenant.[6] The Septuagint translates it with the Greek term *hilasterion*, meaning, "instrument of propitiation." The emphasis was not on its role as a mere cover for the ark but upon its role as the place where atonement takes place ("atonement cover," 25:7 NIV).[7] It is where the children of Israel made peace with God.

The translation "mercy seat" (NASB, KJV, NKJV, RSV etc.) likely comes from Psalm 99:1, "He dwells between the cherubim."[8] It was seen as the throne of God and also as the place to receive God's mercy. God reminded Moses and Aaron of His presence in the Most Holy Place by stating, "I will appear in the cloud above the mercy seat" (Leviticus 16:2). J.R. Porter correctly noted, "It was the divine presence which made the inner sanctuary so holy and so dangerous to enter."[9]

The Preparation (Leviticus 16:3-10)

Preparation was necessary to enter before the ark of the Lord. Verses 3-10 discuss the garments, the animals with which Aaron should enter the Holy Place, and the casting of lots for the goat of sin offering.

• *The Garments.* The high priest was to wear a linen shirt, pants, a sash and a turban when entering the Most Holy Place (Leviticus 16:4). The linen may have been a symbol of purity and holiness.[10] The high priest's regular garments were described in Exodus 28. A quick glance reveals a significant difference between his normal garments and those he wore on the Day of Atonement, which were even simpler than those of the ordinary priests (cf. Exodus 39:27-29). The text does not give an explanation for this. The difference may well be that when a priest appeared before the people he wore the elaborate garments to emphasize his important position as a mediator between God and man ("for glory and for beauty," 28:2). On the Day of Atonement he appeared before God Himself and thus came as a humble servant.[11] Aaron was to bathe before putting on the holy linen garments, symbolizing impurity being washed away.[12]

• *The Animals.* Five animals were required for the people to come into God's presence on the Day of Atonement: a bull, two rams and two goats. A bull without defect was the designated sin offering for a priest (Leviticus 4:3). Wenham calls this offering the "purification offering." Although it atoned for sin, its key emphasis was on purification from the defilement caused by sin.[13] The ram was to be a burnt offering. The most frequent of the sacrifices, the burnt offering was offered at the tabernacle every morning and evening. It is described as a "sweet aroma to the Lord" (1:9). The sin offering focused on purification, but the burnt offering was atonement for sin in general. When sin offerings and burnt offerings were performed together, the sin offering went first.[14] The bull and ram were for the sins and impurities of Aaron and his family.

Two goats were gathered from the people as a sin offering for them. The text does not explain why both goats are said to be a sin offering although only one will actually be sacrificed. It may be because prior to the casting of lots they both were potential sin offerings. The guidelines for sin offerings call for the use of large cattle when sacrificing for the priests and the community as a whole (Leviticus 4:1-21) and the use of small cattle (goats or sheep) when sacrificing for individuals (vv. 22ff). The Day of Atonement is unique in that male goats were used for the community's sacrifices.[15] As was the case with Aaron and his family, a ram was to be sacrificed also as a burnt offering for the people.

• *The Lots.* Leviticus 16:6-10 reveals several key elements of the Day of Atonement. The overall procedure for the day is described in verses 6 and 9. Aaron was to offer the bull for himself and his household before offering the goat for the people. Aaron prepared himself to come into the presence of God before he could intercede on the Israelites' behalf (lest he suffer the same fate as Nadab and Abihu). We are reminded of the words of Jesus, "[W]hy do you look at the speck in your brother's eye, but do not consider the plank in your own eye?" (Matthew 7:3). It is a sobering message to all who find themselves in a position of leadership among God's people.

This section also reveals the process by which one goat was chosen to die and one to live (Leviticus 16:7-10). The animals were placed "before the Lord" (v. 7) and lots were cast. Yahweh chose between them (cf. Acts 1:24-26). This was likely done using the Urim and Thummim (Exodus 28:30; 1 Samuel 28:6).[16] The Mishnah is a written collection of Jewish laws and teachings on observing the Law of Moses that were originally passed on orally. It was compiled sometime between 200 B.C. and A.D. 200 and was divided into 63 divisions or tractates. One of these tractates was called the Yoma and it notes that a red ribbon was placed on the ear of the goat that was to be released (Yoma 4:2)[17], but it is difficult to know the exact process. The important idea is not so much how the goat was chosen, but that God was the one who did the choosing.

Each goat had a purpose. One goat was for the Lord. It was to be sacrificed as a sin offering for the people. The other goat was "for the scapegoat." The term translated as "scapegoat" in the New King James Version is *azazel*. It is found only in Leviticus (16:8, 10, 26). The Hebrew creates a parallel by placing the Hebrew letter *lamed* before Yahweh (i.e., "for the Lord" or "for Yahweh") as well as before *azazel* ("for the scapegoat" or "for azazel"). To determine what is intended by this parallel, we must investigate the meaning of *azazel*.

There are three primary ways of understanding this term. The first says that *azazel* refers to the name of the place where the goat was to be taken, "a fierce, difficult land." This would be seen as a parallel to "an uninhabited land" in Leviticus 16:22.

Another possibility, one adopted by most modern scholars, views this term as the name of a demon ("for Azazel," ASV, RSV). This creates a grammatical parallel with "for Yahweh" and is the most prevalent view of midrashic literature (ancient Jewish commentaries on the Law). The wilderness to which the goat was sent was seen in the ancient world as a habitation of demons (Leviticus 17:7; Matthew 12:43). The apocryphal book of 1 Enoch referred to a rebellious demon called Azel (10:4-5) and is seen as a parallel to the demons in Leviticus 17:7.[18]

The third possibility is to view *azazel* as a reference to the goat itself, a contraction meaning "the goat that goes away." This rendering is found in the Septuagint and the Vulgate and is consistent with the Jewish Mishnah, "the goat which is to be sent forth" (Yoma 6:2).[19] From this understanding we get the rendering "scapegoat" (KJV, NKJV, NIV, NASB).[20] This is probably the best rendering (see endnote).[21]

Conclusion

Whatever the exact meaning of *azazel*, the overall meaning of the ritual involving the live goat is clear. R.K. Harrison states, "The purpose of this very dramatic portion of the day of atonement ritual was to place before the eyes of the Israelites an unmistakable token that their sins of inadvertence had been removed from their midst. It was a symbol of the fact that both people and land had been purged of their guilt."[22]

I like to use visual illustrations periodically in my sermons. For example, I have put mustard on a wedding dress to illustrate the need for purity. I once spoke at a youth gathering while standing in a canoe and talked about Jesus calming the storm on Galilee. Why teach this way? One reason is because God does. He loves to use visual illustrations. Jesus used a small child to teach us about humility. God used visuals in the Old Testament as well. The rituals of the Day of Atonement were, at least in part, visual illustrations of God's sermon on forgiveness. Every sight (the goat being led away), sound (the cries of the animals), and smell (the blood) sent a divine message. They were graphic and living illustrations of the price of sin and what God was doing to forgive Israel and repair the broken relationship between them. I pray we will respond to God's sermon.

Discussion Questions

1. How often have you studied the Day of Atonement before reading this book?

2. How can it be helpful to be aware of the danger of our nature coming in contact with God's nature? Had you ever considered this before?

3. What might we learn from noting the difference in the garments the high priest wore on the Day of Atonement?

Looking Ahead

What does it mean to make atonement?

Chapter 5

The Day of Atonement: Purification

This excerpt is from a speech delivered in the U.S. Senate on Oct. 10, 1995, on the eve of the dedication of Bobby Ray Elementary School in McMinnville, Tenn.:

> A hospital corpsman second class [HC2c] in the U.S. Navy, Bobby Ray served in South Vietnam as a Marine medic. When this country called, he left his home in McMinnville to help his fellow countrymen who were fighting a foreign people on foreign soil. His life was dedicated to saving others, and he always did it with commitment and courage even as gunshots and mortar shells blasted around him.
>
> On March 19, 1969, at the age of 24, Bobby Ray went above and beyond the call of duty. As enemy troops began a heavy assault on the Marines' Battery D, Ray began working on the serious and heavy casualties that fell from rocket and mortar blasts. As he treated a fallen marine, Ray himself became seriously wounded. Refusing medical help, he continued to provide emergency medical treatment to the other casualties. As the enemy drew closer, Ray was forced to battle oncoming soldiers while he administered medical

aid. He did this until he ran out of ammunition and was fatally wounded. But before he died, Bobby Ray performed one more lifesaving act. He threw himself on the last patient he ever treated and saved him from an enemy grenade.

Hospital Corpsman Second Class David Robert Ray gave his own life to save the lives of many others. He became an inspiration to the soldiers in Battery D, who went on to defeat the enemy. For this ultimate sacrifice, the United States awarded Ray the Medal of Honor posthumously.[1]

My children attended Bobby Ray Elementary School, and I pray they never forget his sacrifice. It is the story of one individual sacrificing himself for another. And it is the picture painted on the Day of Atonement in Leviticus 16. If human beings are to live spiritually, there must be a sacrifice.

The book of Leviticus is very important in understanding forgiveness. Leviticus 16 is like the hub of the wheel around which the rest of the book rotates. It summarizes and motivates the book as a whole. In our last chapter we looked at the past and the preparation for the Day of Atonement. Now let us consider the purification and the placement.

The Purification (Leviticus 16:11-28)

Many families have a special time for spring cleaning. Dust collected in the winter months and was missed in the daily and weekly cleaning. The Day of Atonement was similar; it was like a once-a-year spiritual "spring cleaning" for the Israelites. It was a time when they cleansed the tabernacle of any spiritual defilement that had taken place during the year.

Leviticus 16:11 details this process. Having bathed, clothed himself appropriately in linen garments and gathered the proper animals, Aaron was ready to begin the process of purification. The wording at the beginning of verse 11 is the same as at the beginning of verse 6; the significance of this is that Moses gave an overview of the process (vv. 6-10) and then backed up to the beginning and filled in the details (similar to the story of creation told in Genesis 1–2). The order was:

1. Sacrifice of the bull of sin offering (vv. 11-14);

2. Sacrifice of the goat of sin offering (vv. 15-17);
3. The blood rituals (vv. 18-19);
4. The people's scapegoat (vv. 20-22);
5. Sacrifice of rams for burnt offerings (vv. 23-25); and
6. Final washing and disposal (vv. 26-28).

Although some of these elements were covered in the discussion of the previous chapter, a few elements warrant further attention.

Bull of Sin Offering (Leviticus 16:11-14)

Aaron had to make atonement for himself before the community. He began by offering the bull as a sin offering for himself and his family. Two other interesting elements were part of this sacrifice: the incense of protection and the sprinkling of blood.

• *The Incense of Protection.* Aaron took coals from the altar of incense into the Most Holy Place. He placed two handfuls of incense on the coals and the resultant smoke covered the mercy seat. Some believe this was to cover Aaron so God might not see him, the sinner, and destroy him, but it seems clear that the purpose was to cover the presence of God and not the presence of Aaron. The text states, "[T]hat the cloud of incense may cover the mercy seat" (Leviticus 16:13).[2] That was in accordance with God's statement in Exodus 33:20, "You cannot see My face; for no man shall see Me, and live." We are again reminded of the danger of God's presence.

• *The Sprinkling of Blood.* The sprinkling of blood was very similar to the procedure used with the regular sin offering for a priest (Leviticus 4:3ff). The main difference was the location at which the blood was sprinkled. During a regular sin offering, it was sprinkled on the veil separating the Holy Place from the Most Holy Place (v. 6). On the Day of Atonement, the blood was taken into the very presence of the Lord in the Most Holy Place. Baruch Levine states that the blood was sprinkled once over the mercy seat and then seven times in front of it. "The first sprinkling was done with an upward motion and the other seven sprinklings, with a downward motion."[3] The number seven is the most frequent of the symbolic numbers used in the Bible and is found in nearly 600 passages as a symbol of totality or completeness.[4] It is worth noting that in the Levitical sacrifices the location at which the blood is sprinkled is determined by the proximity of the worshiper to God (cf. the camp layout we referred to earlier). The closer the worshiper was allowed to come to God, the closer the blood was sprinkled. For the common people it was sprinkled on the altar in the courtyard. For the priests it was sprinkled on the veil between the Holy and Most Holy Places. Finally, on the Day of Atonement, the high priest placed it on the ark itself (1:5; 4:6).

Goat of Sin Offering (Leviticus 16:15-17)

Aaron followed the same procedure with the people's goat of sin offering as he had with his own bull. Only the high priest was to be within the tent during this event. Aaron was engaged in a very dangerous activity; it was imperative that all others stay away or death would be the consequence. "So he shall make atonement for the Holy Place, because of the uncleanness of the children of Israel, and because of their transgressions, for all their sins; and so he shall do for the tabernacle of meeting which remains among them in the midst of their uncleanness" (Leviticus 16:16). The sins and impurities of the people defiled God's dwelling place. The only way a holy God could dwell among a sinful people was if their sins and impurities had been atoned for and the tabernacle had been cleansed. Levine stresses that the purity of God's dwelling place had to be maintained. "In a very real sense, this was the primary purpose of the entire biblical ritual of Yom Kippur."[5]

The Blood Rituals (Leviticus 16:18-20)

The blood of animals is emphasized again, and its significance is described in Leviticus 17:11, "For the life of the flesh is in the blood, and I have given it to you upon the altar to make atonement for your souls; for it is the blood that makes atonement for the soul." The term *kipper*, "atonement," is found 16 times in chapter 16 and 33 times elsewhere in Leviticus.[6] Its meaning is difficult, for it seems to be used in two different ways: "ransom" and "cleansing." In the sacrificial system, the animal is the ransom the condemned man pays to redeem his life, signified in the shedding of blood. The blood also serves to cleanse the tabernacle and worshipers from the defilements of impurity and sin.[7]

People's Scapegoat (Leviticus 16:20-22)

Two elements concerning the scapegoat are worthy of further notice. The first is the laying on of hands. The text states, "Aaron shall lay both his hands on the head of the live goat, confess over it all the iniquities of the children of Israel" (Leviticus 16:21). M.C. Sansom, in his detailed study of the laying on of hands in the Old Testament, notices two primary purposes for this ritual: identification and transference. The laying on of a single hand by the worshiper prior to the burnt, peace and sin offerings seemed to be for the purpose of identifying the animal as the one to take the worshiper's place. Transference of sin could not be involved, else the animal could not be placed on the altar because it would be unclean. The laying on of both hands on the Day of Atonement was for the purpose of transference. The sins of the people were figuratively transferred to the goat. This unclean goat was then sent outside the camp with the other unclean things. Sansom notes that some significance may be found in the use of one hand (identity) or two hands (transference).[8]

This ritual is an object lesson of the removal of sins. The goat was taken to an "uninhabited place," probably to ensure that it did not wander back into the camp. In later times the goat was taken to a desolate place and pushed over a cliff backwards to insure that it did not return (Mishnah Yoma 6:6).[9] The sacrificial goat and the live goat give a two-fold picture of atonement: ransom (sacrificed goat) and removal (scapegoat). The live goat is a vivid picture of Psalm 103:12, "As far as the east is from the west, So far has He removed our transgressions from us."

Rams for Burnt Offerings (Leviticus 16:23-25)

Until this point the high priest had been in the tent alone (Leviticus 16:17). It was a dangerous time for the priest and likely involved tense moments for the people. There must have been a tremendous sense of relief and joy when the high priest reemerged to offer the burnt offerings. He had to remove the linen garments, bathe and don his regular garments before doing so. The linen garments had been "infected with holiness" and "had to remain in a holy place so that no one would be in danger of coming in contact with them."[10] The cleansing may have been to remove the holiness which Aaron had contacted.[11] Aaron was no longer entering the Most Holy Place as a lowly servant. He was now back before the people to perform the burnt offering, so he wore the regular garments that indicated his position as mediator between God and man.

Final Washing and Disposal (Leviticus 16:26-28)

The final washing and disposal of animal remains were in keeping with Leviticus 4. Both the one who released the goat and the one who burned the remains of the sin offerings had to bathe before re-entering the camp. Each had become ceremonially unclean by contacting the people's sins. "Through the entire ceremony the emphasis is upon the holiness of God as contrasted with the sin of man, and the necessity for the worshiper ... to follow scrupulously the directions for approaching God in worship." [12]

Placement (Leviticus 16:29-34)

Having made atonement for the priests, the people, the sanctuary and the altar, one problem remained – the atonement would not last. The people would sin again, and the sanctuary would be polluted again. Thus, there was a need for repeated cleansing (an annual spiritual spring cleaning). God dealt with this problem by making the Day of Atonement a permanent statute (Leviticus 16:29, 31). It was placed in the Jewish calender on the 10th day of the seventh month. After the exile, this month would be known as Tishri and corresponds to September-October in the modern calendar. It was the time of the year when the rains fell and the land was plowed and prepared for the planting that would begin the next month.[13] Sadly, the children of Israel failed to honor this command.

The people were told, "humble your souls" during this time (Leviticus 16:29, 31). The phrase is translated as "afflict yourselves" (NKJV, ASV, RSV) or "deny yourselves" (NIV). The phrase is also traditionally understood to mean "fasting" (TEV), parallel with fasting in Psalm 35:13 and Isaiah 58:3. It also carried with it the idea of repentance.[14] The Israelites had to do more than perform a ritual. They had to be penitent for their sins and impurities. The fasting and Sabbath rest allowed them to focus on their sins and the holiness of their God. Understanding their actions should inspire us to take time in our schedules to do the same.

Conclusion

Many Americans died fighting in Afghanistan and Iraq. Pat Tillman was one of them. He left a successful career in the National Football League and a multi-million dollar salary to fight for his country. The images of the burning buildings and crashing planes that he saw on Sept. 11, 2001, compelled him to leave everything and fight so that others would not die. No one forced him; he went willingly. He sacrificed his life to save others.

The animals sacrificed on the Day of Atonement saved people from their sins, but the animals did not die willingly and their sacrifices would never be enough (Hebrews 10:1-4). Therefore, God the Son left the glory of heaven and come to earth so that He might give His life to save all humanity from their sins. John Hartley correctly summarizes, "Jesus' death has thus accomplished the full intent of both the Day of Atonement and the whole sacrificial system." [15] His atoning death both "ransomed" and "cleansed" the believer from his sins. It is this story of sacrifice that we will explore in the chapters to come. I hope that the atonement we read about in Leviticus 16 has opened our eyes to the legacy of sin. I pray that the atonement we will see at calvary will transform our lives into the likeness of the Son.

Discussion Questions

1. Are you glad we are not under the sacrificial system? Why?

2. How would it make you feel to watch one of your sheep die for your sins? Do you think it helped the Israelites to understand the cost of sin?

3. How does the image of the scapegoat help us to understand forgiveness?

Looking Ahead

How is it helpful to consider forgiveness in the Old Testament before proceeding to the New Testament?

Chapter 6

Graduation

The launching of the space shuttle Discovery on July 26, 2005 was very significant. It was the first launch after the explosion of the space shuttle Columbia. It symbolized that America would not quit. The message of the Old Testament has shown us that God keeps launching His plan. Human beings may crash and burn, but God never quits.

We often think of the Old Testament as a relic of the past that has little, if any, relevance for us. That is not the case. Nearly one out of every 10 of Jesus' recorded words in the New Testament either cites or alludes to the Old Testament.[1] Paul said, "For whatever things were written before were written for our learning" (Romans 15:4). The Law supervised and prepared humanity for the coming of Christ and the system of faith. From the very first words of Genesis, we begin to learn about the nature of God, humanity and the creation.

Thus far in our study we have been focusing on the "tutor." Yet, just as we graduate from high school and move on to college or careers, so it is time in our study to move on to Christ and the message of the New Testament. Terry Briley notes that some view the Old Testament like the solid rocket boosters on the space shuttle that are jettisoned when no longer needed. He says that the Law is more like an elementary math class that we move on from but do not want to forget.[2] We still benefit from knowing that 1+1=2 when we are taking college algebra. Now let us see how God continues to launch His plan in the New Testament. This chapter is designed to give us a "shuttle's-eye view" of the New Testament terms and teaching on forgiveness.

Nouns for Forgiveness in the New Testament

Our study of the Old Testament terms for forgiveness gave a nice overview of the subject, and we will be benefitted by focusing briefly on the New Testament terms as well. We begin with the noun *aphesis* (**a**-fes-is).[3] This term is found 17 times in the New Testament, 10 of which are found in Luke and Acts.[4] It comes from a root that means "to send away."[5] It is used in the Septuagint in Leviticus 16:26 to refer to the goat sent away into the wilderness to bear the sins of the people on the Day of Atonement.[6] *Aphesis* means "a) Release from bondage or imprisonment, or b) Forgiveness or pardon of sins (letting them go as if they had never been committed), remission (forgiveness) of the penalty."[7] Jesus uses the term in Matthew 26:28, "For this is My blood of the new covenant, which is shed for many for the remission of sins."[8] The key is that the blood of Christ makes it possible for us to avoid the punishment we deserve for our sins. It is as if our sins had never been committed. This relates to the idea of the "blotting out of sin" seen in Psalm 51. The punishment is removed because the crime is removed.

The noun *paresis* (**pa**-re-sis) is used only in Romans 3:25, "[W]hom God set forth as a propitiation by His blood, through faith, to demonstrate His righteousness, because in His forbearance God had *passed over* the sins that were previously committed" (italics mine).

"Paul uses *paresis* instead of the usual *aphesis*. The former means 'putting aside,' 'disregarding,' 'pretermission'; the latter, 'putting away' completely and unreservedly. It does not mean forgiveness in the complete sense."[9] This term signifies that something was lacking in the forgiveness of the Old Law. That "something" was Jesus Christ ("a propitiation"). "Propitiation" in verse 25 is the Greek term *hilasteerion* (hi-la-**stay**-ree-on). Its only other New Testament usage is in Hebrews 9:5, where it is used to describe the "mercy seat" in the Tabernacle.[10] *The Theological Dictionary of the New Testament* comments on *aphesis* and *paresis*: "The forgiveness denoted is almost always that of God. It is constantly needed, and is granted when requested so long as there is a readiness to forgive others. Its basis is the saving act of Christ." [11]

Verbs in the New Testament

The favorite verb in the Gospels for "to forgive" is *aphiemi* (a-**fee**-e-mi). It is frequently used in the Septuagint to translate the Hebrew verb *calach*.[12] *Aphiemi* means "to send away" in the sense of "to let go, give up, a debt, by not demanding it," [13] so was used for the cancelling of a debt. It is often translated as "leave" or "let" in addition to "forgive" or "be forgiven." W.E. Vine states that the verb *aphiemi* "firstly signifies the remission of the punishment due to sinful conduct, the deliverance of the sinner from the penalty divinely, and therefore righteously, imposed; secondly, it involves the complete removal of the cause of offense; such remission is based upon the vicarious and propitiatory sacrifice of Christ." [14] Jesus used it in Matthew 9:6, "But that you may know that the Son of Man has power on earth *to forgive* sins" (emphasis mine).

The next verb, *charidzomai* (kha-**ri**-dzo-mai), is found 24 times in the New Testament and 17 times in Paul's writings. This is Paul's favorite verb for "to forgive." It is often translated simply as "to give" or "to grant" (cf. Romans 8:32).[15] It comes from *charis,* which means "graciousness." [16] *Charidzomai* refers to a gracious act, "to grant forgiveness, to pardon." [17] Paul uses the term in Ephesians 4:32, "And be kind to one another, tenderhearted, *forgiving* one another, even as God in Christ *forgave* you" (emphasis mine). It is not surprising that this would be a favorite term of Paul in light of the emphasis he places on God's grace (cf. Romans 3:24; 1 Corinthians 1:3; 2 Corinthians 1:2; etc.). This word helps to express the emphasis Paul placed on the graciousness of God's pardon.[18] The only time it is translated as "to forgive" in the Gospels is in Luke 7:42-43 when Jesus responded to the Pharisee's comments about the sinful woman who washed Jesus' feet.

Another verb to note is *apoluo* (a-po-**loo**-o). It means "to set free, to let go, to release." [19] It is used in regard to captives, prisoners or debtors who are released from their bonds, punishment or debt. It is even used to describe divorce and the "putting away" of a husband or wife. It is found in Luke 6:37, "Judge not, and you shall not be judged. Condemn not, and you shall not be condemned. *Forgive*, and you will be *forgiven*" (emphasis mine). This is the only place where *apoluo* is translated as "forgiven." It is used here because Jesus is comparing sin to a debt that one is released from.[20] Releasing another is a response of mercy motivated by the mercy of God (cf. Luke 6:36). *Aphiemi* and *apoluo* are used together in the parable of the unmerciful servant in Matthew 18:26-28, "Then the master of that servant was moved with compassion, released [*apoluo*] him, and forgave [*aphiemi*] him the debt."[21]

A verb which sounds similar to *apoluo*, but is different in meaning, is *apolouo* (a-po-**loo**-o). This verb means "to wash off or to wash away,"[22] and it is used in Acts 22:16, "And now why are you waiting? Arise and be baptized, and *wash away* your sins, calling on the name of the Lord." *Apolouo* reminds us of the numerous references to washing and cleansing that we noted in our study of Old Testament terms (Psalm 51).

New Testament Teaching

Luke serves as a good learning tool on forgiveness for several reasons: he connects forgiveness to the message of the Old Testament (Luke 24:44-48); he connects forgiveness to the ministry of Jesus; he connects forgiveness to the history of the early church; and he connects forgiveness to the ministry of Paul.[23] He can help us to pull together the Old and New Testament teachings on the forgiveness of sins. Forgiveness in the Old Testament focused primarily on God's forgiveness of human beings. The Old Testament says a great deal about how humans are to treat each other, but very little about humans forgiving each other. The New Testament reveals new facets of forgiveness like a diamond which sparkles and glistens anew as it rotates in the light.

Key Person: Jesus

In the first part of his gospel, Luke described the coming of John the Baptist and John's work – bringing the knowledge of the "forgiveness of sins" (Luke 1:77; 3:3). John achieved his purpose through his teaching, the practice of baptism for the forgiveness of sins, and paving the way for Jesus. Luke also presented Jesus as the key to forgiveness: Jesus brought forgiveness to humanity (Acts 5:31). He has the power to forgive sins (Luke 5:20-24; 7:47-50). He proclaimed the message of forgiveness (4:16-21), which takes place in Jesus' name (Acts 2:38; 10:43). After Jesus returned to heaven, the disciples were to proclaim "forgiveness of sins" in His name, starting at Jerusalem (Luke 24:47; Acts 13:38-39; 26:18). Finally, He is depicted as the ultimate example of forgiveness (Luke 23:34; 7:37-43). Luke proclaimed that there is no forgiveness without Christ.

Key Passage: Luke 24

Luke's (and Christ's) view of forgiveness is summed up in Luke 24:44-49. The passage connects the work of Christ with the message of the Old Testament (v. 44). It connects Christ's death to the preaching of the remission of sins (v. 47). Although Luke stressed that Jesus' death was necessary and that His life pointed toward Jerusalem and the cross, he did not place emphasis on the atoning nature of Christ's death as Matthew, Mark and Paul did (Matthew 26:28; 1 Corinthians 11:23-26). However, we should not view this as evidence that he did not believe Christ's death atoned for our sins. Two key passages to examine are Luke 22:19-20 and Acts 20:28, passages that sound similar to statements made by Paul (1 Corinthians 11:23-26). Luke 22:19-20 involved the institution of the Lord's Supper. It echoed Isaiah 53 and Jeremiah 31 and emphasized the atoning nature Christ's death.

• *Atonement in Luke.* Luke and Paul worked together, as denoted by the "we" sections of Acts, and were inspired by the same Holy Spirit. In fact, many parts of Acts describe Paul's activities and words to the people he encountered. For example, Acts 20:28 was spoken by Paul to the Ephesian elders. This verse stressed that redemption came through Jesus' blood by using the imagery of a slave ransomed and set free. Paul's words are consistent with Colossians 1:14, which connects redemption (*apolutrosis*) with forgiveness (*aphesis*). The Old Testament echoes in Acts 20:28 as well – in Psalm 74:2 and Isaiah 43:21, the Greek version of the Old Testament uses the same verb that is translated as "purchased" in Acts 20:28.[24] Notice the stress placed on Christ's dying for the collective body; this is consistent with the emphasis in Acts on the fellowship experienced as the "called out ones." Salvation makes us part of something, the kingdom of God.

• *Forgiveness Proclaimed.* Luke 24 contains the proclamation of repentance and forgiveness of sins that was to go forth from Jerusalem and played out on the Day of Pentecost (Acts 2). The events of that day tie it back to Luke 24 as well as back to the message of the prophets. Peter quoted from the prophet Joel and applied it to Pentecost (Joel 2:28-32; Acts 2:17-21). He told the crowd, "[R]epent, and let every one of you be baptized in the name of Jesus Christ for the remission of sins; and you shall receive the gift of the Holy Spirit" (v. 38). The message of forgiveness in the name of Christ went forth from Jerusalem just as Jesus directed (Luke 24:44-49).

Key Point: All

Luke stressed that salvation and forgiveness are available to all (Luke 2:29-32; 19:10; 24:47; Acts 1:6-8; 2:21, etc.). Remember that the Old Testament narrative primarily focused on the forgiveness of Israel but hinted at a salvation that would be available to all. This concept is found in God's promise to Abram that He would bless all nations (Genesis 12:1-3). It is found in Joel's prophecy that Peter quotes in Acts 2:21, "And it shall come to pass That whoever calls on the name of the Lord Shall be saved" (cf. Joel 2:32). It is found in Acts 15:16-17 where James, the brother of our Lord, quoted from Amos 9:11-12: "After this I will return And will rebuild the tabernacle of David, which has fallen down; I will rebuild its ruins, And I will set it up; So that the rest of mankind may seek the Lord, Even all the Gentiles who are called by My name, Says the Lord who does all these things." Acts 15 is a discussion of the role of Gentiles in the church and the question of whether they must be circumcised. The Old Testament prophets prophesied the restoration of Israel, the gathering of a remnant, and the rebuilding of the tabernacle (Ezekiel 40ff). Amos prophesied that when this happened, the Gentiles would be included. James confirmed that what the prophets foretold had taken place, saying that all nations had come into Israel through the church.

This notion harkens back to the list of nations in Acts 2:5-11; these people are the restoration of Israel. One sees a consistent pattern in Acts (1:6-8). The early evangelists began by restoring Israel (Acts 2) and then moved on to the Gentiles (Acts 10ff). They went "to the Jew first and also to the Greek" (Romans 1:16). This is consistent with Paul's habit of evangelizing each city by going first to the Jewish synagogue and moving outward. All nations are therefore blessed.

Key Process: Conversion

Luke also revealed how one should respond to the forgiveness of God. He stressed that the forgiven should love the Lord and respond out of gratitude for what He has done for them (Luke 7:37-43). Luke described how the forgiveness of sins is received – through faith (Acts 10:43), repentance (before baptism, Luke 3:3; Acts 2:38; after baptism, 8:22), baptism (Luke 3:3; Acts 2:38; 22:16), and prayer (Luke 11:1-4; Acts 8:22). Luke conveyed a strong bond between the forgiveness of sins and baptism (Luke 3:3; Acts 2:38). Many try to work around this bond, but they cannot do so and honor the text of Luke. The reception of forgiveness and the Spirit are connected as well (2:38; 19:1-6). A connection is consistent with the fact that the church is the rebuilt temple of God in which the Spirit dwells (15:16-17; 1 Corinthians 3:16-17).

The forgiven are called to forgive others (Luke 7:37-43; 11:4; 17:3-4). This call to forgive others is a new facet from the teachings of the Old Testament. The Old Testament stressed proper treatment of others (Leviticus 19:18), but the New Testament emphasizes that we should forgive others.

Conclusion

One fact is driven home by the writings of Luke and the rest of the New Testament, "The God of our fathers raised up Jesus whom you murdered by hanging on a tree. Him God has exalted to His right hand to be Prince and Savior, to give repentance to Israel and forgiveness of sins" (Acts 5:30-31). Have you ever been to Rock City in Chattanooga, Tenn.? Even if you have not, my guess is that you have seen a sign pointing you there. You were probably driving down the road and saw a barn roof that said, "See Rock City." People all over the country and world know about Rock City because of those roofs. Are you searching for something spiritually? Would you like to find peace? Are you trying to find the way to forgiveness? There are signs all over the "roofs" of God's Word proclaiming, "See Jesus Christ." He is where forgiveness is found!

Discussion Questions

1. Name three things you learned from studying the New Testament words for forgiveness?

2. Do you think Luke is a good choice as an author to focus on as we seek to gain insight into the New Testament view of forgiveness?

3. Who else might we have chosen, and why would you choose him?

Looking Ahead

What would you be willing to do to bring peace to the world?

Chapter 7

Peace
With God

C olonel Terry "Max" Haston spoke at the Armed Forces Day ceremony in McMinnville, Tenn., on May 18, 2002. He stated that he had taken a copy of the Wall Street journal and circled every mention of a conflict somewhere in the world. He found 42 wars or conflicts. It seems that every day we read of new terrorist attacks and fighting from New York City to Tel Aviv, Israel. Conflicts are also in congregations, neighborhoods and even families.

Into this den of madness, Paul shouts, "Therefore, having been justified by faith, we have peace with God through our Lord Jesus Christ" (Romans 5:1). The answer to peace with my fellowman, peace with my brother, peace with my struggles, and peace with my guilt lies in understanding the concept of "peace with God." Having focused on how God showed forgiveness under the Law of Moses, we can now move to how He has shown it in Christ. In the next two chapters we will focus on atonement and redemption as seen in Christ's death on the cross. This chapter will examine the role Christ has played in making peace. We will explore in further detail why sin results in a lost relationship with God and how the One we have treated as an enemy has become our friend.

The Past

Let us go for a moment back to the Gospel of Luke. The theme passage for Luke and Acts might well be Luke 4:16-21:

> So He came to Nazareth, where He had been brought up. And as His custom was, He went into the synagogue on the Sabbath day, and stood up to read. And He was handed the book of the prophet Isaiah. And when He had opened the book, He found the place where it was written: "The Spirit of the Lord is upon Me, Because He has anointed Me To preach the gospel to the poor; He has sent Me to heal the brokenhearted, To proclaim liberty [*aphesis*] to the captives And recovery of sight to the blind, To set at liberty [*aphesis*] those who are oppressed; To proclaim the acceptable year of the Lord." Then He closed the book, and gave it back to the attendant and sat down. And the eyes of all who were in the synagogue were fixed on Him. And He began to say to them, "Today this Scripture is fulfilled in your hearing."

Verses 18-19 are a paraphrase of Isaiah 61:1-2 and 58:6. Isaiah 61 alludes to the year of Jubilee (Leviticus 25:8-55) when debts were canceled, slaves were freed, and property was returned. Joel Green notes several reasons why this passage in Luke is important: it represents the first spoken words of Jesus in the Gospel as an adult; it is the only place in Luke where the content of His synagogue teaching is given; it is later referred to in Luke and the book of Acts as evidence that Jesus is the Christ (Luke 7:18-23; Acts 10:38); and it is at the beginning of His public ministry.[1]

Green also notes the emphasis the original Greek places on the words "me" and "release" by putting them at the end of the phrases they are found in.[2] Bringing together the elements learned from our study of forgiveness thus far, this passage stresses that Jesus' work is part of the master plan of God ("Spirit"; "He anointed me"). His role as the proclaimer and provider of liberty is emphasized. "Liberty" is a translation of the Greek term *aphesis*, which we noted earlier is the key New Testament noun for forgiveness.[3] "Liberty" alludes to more than release from physical difficulties; it is also a metaphor for liberty from sin. This liberty is for all: poor, captive, blind and oppressed. Consistent with the emphasis Luke places on the availability of salvation for all humanity (Luke 2:29-32; 19:10; 24:47; Acts 1:6-8; 2:21), these verses can also serve as a bridge to the teaching of Paul. Paul later elaborated on why humanity needed the salvation Christ proclaimed and how He provided it.

The Peace of God

Have you ever looked at the moon through a telescope? It is both fascinating and peaceful. In 1969, Neil Armstrong and Buzz Aldrin placed a plaque on the moon in a region called the Sea of Tranquility. The plaque reads, "We come in peace for all mankind."[4] The moon is a peaceful place, but it is only so because few humans have been there. Where human beings go, there is little peace. It is no different when God is involved. We struggle to have peace with Him as well. Yet, Romans 5:1 says, "[W]e have peace with God." To understand what it means to have peace with God, we need to consider what it means to be the enemy of God.

Peace is often lost between people and nations when one hurts the other or when one breaks an agreement made between the parties. We have done that to God – it is called "sin." In Romans 3:10 and 3:23 Paul states that all people sin. No one is exempt. Sin is called "lawlessness" in 1 John 3:4. Sins are human acts that violate the laws of God and thus make us enemies of God. Isaiah 59:1-2 states, "Behold, the Lord's hand is not shortened, That it cannot save; Nor His ear heavy, That it cannot hear. But your iniquities have separated you from your God; And your sins have hidden His face from you, So that He will not hear." Paul states in Romans 2:5-9 that God "will render to each one according to his deeds" and that this includes "indignation and wrath, tribulation and anguish, on every soul of man who does evil."

We may ask, "How can this be? I thought God was a merciful God." He *is* a merciful God. He is not, however, a one-dimensional God. Notice what Paul says in Romans 11:22: "Therefore consider the goodness and severity of God: on those who fell, severity; but toward you, goodness, if you continue in His goodness. Otherwise you also will be cut off." Kindness and severity are both attributes of God (Exodus 34:7). He is a God of justice and mercy. Many problems existing in the church and the religious world at large stem from a basic failure to understand this.

God's nature demands that sinners become enemies of God. "God is light and in Him is no darkness at all" (1 John 1:5). He "cannot be tempted by evil" (James 1:13). Revelation 21:27 states of heaven, "But there shall by no means enter it anything that defiles, or causes an abomination or a lie, but only those who are written in the Lamb's Book of Life." God is good. Just as oil and water do not mix, God and sin do not mix. His nature repels evil. Why do we bury the dead? Is it because we do not love them? No. It is because we have different natures. The living and the dead cannot co-exist. Likewise, God and the sinner cannot co-exist. It is not because He does not love us (John 3:16). It is because our natures are different.

God is not only good; He is just. Paul stressed this righteousness in Romans 3–4. If God is righteous, He must be just. Romans 2:16 states, "God will judge the secrets of men by Christ Jesus," who is the "righteous Judge" (2 Timothy 4:8). If He is a righteous judge, He must punish sin. Imagine that someone murdered a loved one of yours. If that person was caught and taken before a judge, how would you feel if the judge said to the perpetrator, "Don't worry about. It was your first murder. You just go on home"? Would you consider that judge to be just and fair? Of course not! Would you want to live in a society where crimes went unpunished? No way! If God does not punish sin, He ceases to be just.

Sinners must therefore be enemies of God. We are all sinners. We are headed for hell and powerless to do anything about it. We are drowning in sin and cannot save ourselves. Hebrews 10:31 teaches, "It is a fearful thing to fall into the hands of the living God."

Still, Paul states, "[W]e have peace with God" (Romans 5:1). There is a textual debate over whether this should read "We have peace with God" or "Let us have peace with God." The context of the passage supports the former rendering. Paul is referring to something we possess. In light of what we have just learned, how can this be? How can we have peace with God? That is where the peacemaker comes in.

The Peacemaker

Every year on December 10 the Nobel Peace prize is awarded to no more than three people who have played a significant role in promoting peace in the world during the preceding year. The prize was first awarded in 1901 to the Swiss founder of the Red Cross and a

Frenchman who was the founder and president of the first French peace society. It has been given to people like Albert Schweitzer (1952), Martin Luther King Jr. (1964), and Mother Teresa (1979).[5] Despite the great accomplishments of these people, their efforts for peace pale in comparison to the greatest peacemaker of all time – Jesus, our Lord!

God's justice demanded that He punish sin, but His love was "not willing that any should perish" (2 Peter 3:9). How could God reconcile this problem and be at peace with mankind? "[W]e have peace with God through our Lord Jesus Christ" (Romans 5:1). Jesus is the answer.

A king once made a decree that all those in his kingdom convicted of stealing would have two eyes plucked out. One day the king's own son was brought before the king for stealing. Justice demanded that the king punish his son; his credibility would be shattered if he let his son go free. But he did not want his son to be blind for the rest of his life. The king decided to take one of his son's eyes and one of his own. He punished the sin – he was a just king. He also paid the price himself – he was a loving father. God the Father must punish sin – He is a just King. But Jesus also paid the price for us because God is a loving Father. He took the punishment upon Himself that we might be reconciled (Romans 5:8-11). The only difference between the story of the king and what God did for us is that God gave both eyes. We are totally unworthy of salvation or peace (Ephesians 2:3), but the "God of peace" stepped in and saved us. He took our place (Romans 15:3).

To understand fully what has taken place, let us look at the word "justified" in Romans 5:1. As a passive verb, we know that we do not justify ourselves, but it is something done to us. Bauer's lexicon defines "justified" as to "be acquitted, be pronounced and treated as righteous."[6] Paul is not saying we are righteous. He is saying we are treated as if we were righteous. "For what does the Scripture say? 'Abraham believed God, and it was accounted to him for righteousness' " (4:3). Based on his faith, Abraham was "treated" or "accounted" as if he were righteous, although he was not. The same is true for us (vv. 23-25). Our spiritual bank account was empty, but Christ made a deposit for us. His righteousness was "accounted" to our spiritual bank account. Christ took the penalty of our sins so that we could be acquitted or set free from our sins. Justification means Jesus was treated "just as if" He had lived my life, so that I can be treated "just as if" I had lived His life. God vented His righteous wrath on Jesus, and Jesus received what we deserved so that we can receive what He deserves. God's justice has now been satisfied. We can be reconciled to God and enjoy His love. We have "peace with God."

The message of the book of Romans, and more specifically Romans 5:1, is that God is the peacemaker. The word "God" is found more frequently in Romans than in any other letter Paul wrote. In contrast, the words "Christ" and "Jesus Christ" are found less frequently than in Paul's other writings. This is not to say that Christ is not central to the book (our text makes it evident that He is). The stress instead is being placed on what the Father is doing through Christ. This is consistent with the God we saw in the pages of the Old Testament. God was taking action on the behalf of humanity to make peace. The irony is that the one who should be our enemy has become our peacemaker.

Conclusion

Ralph Turnbull tells of a friend who visited an elderly woman badly crippled by arthritis. His friend asked her, "Do you suffer much?" "Yes, but there is no nail here," she responded as she pointed to her hand. "He had the nails, I have the peace." She then pointed to her head. "There are no thorns here. He had the thorns, I have the peace." She touched her side and said, "There is no spear here. He had the spear, I have the peace." [7] On the cross of Calvary, Jesus had the pain; we have the peace!

Discussion Questions

1. Can you think of some Bible stories of people who were the enemies of God?

2. What happened to nations in the Old Testament that were enemies of God? How should this reality make us feel about our sin?

3. Can you think of someone who helped you work out peacefully a problem that existed between you and another person? How do you feel toward this peacemaker?

Looking Ahead

What does the Day of Atonement have to do with Jesus?

Chapter 8

Watch
the Lamb

Several years ago I was able to hear a Christian college chorus sing a song called "Watch the Lamb." Written from the perspective of Simon of Cyrene, the song describes Simon traveling to Jerusalem with his two sons and a small lamb for the Passover feast. The job of the two sons is to "watch the lamb" they were to sacrifice in Jerusalem. The journey turns from a time of worship and celebration into a trip of terror as the family find themselves caught up in the terrible events surrounding the cross. Simon describes the brutally beaten Jesus and the screaming crowd. He details the horror of having to carry the cross and feeling the blood of Jesus as it drops and runs down Simon's cheek.

Simon's heart is touched as he hears the words "Father forgive them" and sees the look of love in the eyes of the Savior. The song ends with Simon and his sons standing beneath the cross where the lifeless body of Jesus hangs. The boys are weeping because they let the little lamb get away. They are confused and afraid and want to know what is happening around them. Their dad picks them up and they turn to face the cross. Simon tells the boys to "watch the Lamb." [1] The boys did not need their lamb anymore because God had provided one.

There were few dry eyes in the audience when the song ended. When hearts are given a glimpse of the Lamb of God, they often break.

In the last chapter we explored the role Christ played in repairing our relationship with God. In this lesson we will focus on Christ as the atoning sacrifice for sin. We are seeking the anti-venom to conquer the power of Satan's poison. The key is to "watch the Lamb"! We will focus on the sacrifice and the Savior as we "watch the Lamb."

Sacrifice of the Lamb

Abram had marched from his homeland with God's promise of a great land, a great nation, and a great blessing echoing in his mind (Genesis 12). That same hope buoyed Abram's descendants Isaac, Jacob and Joseph, but by the time of the events recorded in Exodus 3, that hope was gone. Four hundred years of slavery had ground it into the Egyptian sand. Hundreds of miles away a simple shepherd stood on a mountainside staring at a bush that burned but was not consumed. While God's people labored under the taskmasters' whips, this shepherd, whom God had been training for 80 years, reluctantly obeyed God's command: "[B]ring My people, the children of Israel, out of Egypt" (Exodus 3:10). Help was on the way!

Ethan was afraid. Ethan was excited. Ethan was eight years old. He lived in the land of Goshen in Egypt. Like his father before him, he was the son of a slave. He was the oldest child of his parents. Strange things had been happening since the arrival of Moses. Plague after plague had come upon the Egyptians: water turned to blood, frogs, lice, flies, dead cattle, boils, hail, locusts, darkness and now … death of the firstborn. Ethan was a firstborn! He heard that the Lord's angel was coming that night. It was drawing close to midnight. Would the destroyer come soon? Would he be spared? Ethan's father saw the worried look on his face and said, "You are safe, my son; the blood of the lamb is upon the lintel and doorposts of our home. The blood will save you, and we will be delivered this night from the hands of the Egyptians. The Lord commanded us to eat while standing so that we might leave quickly." Suddenly Ethan heard a noise outside and felt a chill run up his spine. It lasted for only a moment and then passed. Thank God for the lamb!

The story of Ethan is only make-believe, but it fits the events recorded in Exodus 12–13. God commanded the people to sacrifice a perfect, unblemished lamb. They were to eat the meat without breaking the bones. They were to spread the blood on the doorposts and lintels of their homes. If the death angel saw the blood on the door, he would pass over the home and spare the firstborn. God delivered His people from bondage in Egypt and they were to observe this Passover meal each year to commemorate the event (Exodus 13:1-10). Sacrifice became central to the Israelites' worship of God. Lambs and young rams were a vital part of almost every sacrifice in the Old Testament (Leviticus 4:32; Numbers 6:14).

Leviticus 1–7 details the five key sacrifices: the burnt offering for general sin, the grain offering for commitment to God, the peace offering for gratitude and communion with God, the sin offering for purification, and the guilt offering for repaying those wronged by sin (God and man). The Israelites learned that the shedding of blood was necessary to save one from death. Countless lambs died because of the sins of humanity, but their blood was not enough (Hebrews 10:4). Isaiah foretold of another Lamb who would come:

> All we like sheep have gone astray; We have turned, every one, to his own way; And the Lord has laid on Him the iniquity of us all. He was oppressed and He was afflicted, Yet He opened not His mouth; He was led as a lamb to the slaughter, And as a sheep before its shearers is silent, So He opened not His mouth (53:6-7).

Savior of the World

In a lonely manger in Bethlehem, unknown to most of the world, a baby boy was born to a young couple from the insignificant city of Nazareth. In a place where animals were fed and cared for, the Lamb of God came into the world. The first ones to know of this great event were men who cared for sheep; an angel spoke kind words to those shepherds, "Do not be afraid, for behold, I bring you good tidings of great joy which will be to all people. For there is born to you this day in the city of David a Savior, who is Christ the Lord" (Luke 2:10-11). Help was on the way!

In Luke 2:22-24, Mary and Joseph took baby Jesus to Jerusalem to offer a sacrifice in accordance with the Law of Moses. The law called for a lamb and a turtledove or pigeon as a purification offering. If a family was poor, they were required to sacrifice only two turtledoves or pigeons (Leviticus 12:6-8). Isn't it ironic that the Lamb of God was born into a family too poor to afford a lamb for sacrifice? As sinners, we are too poor to afford the Lamb of God. He came as a gift from above (Romans 6:23).

In John 1:29 John the Baptist declared that the Lamb of God "takes away the sin of the world." "Again, the next day, John stood with two of his disciples. And looking at Jesus as He walked, he said, 'Behold the Lamb of God!' The two disciples heard him speak, and they followed Jesus" (John 1:35-37). John the Baptist was one of a kind (Matthew 11:11). He was a man of the wilderness who did not wear fine clothing or eat delicate food. He wore camel hair garments and dined on locusts and wild honey (3:4). He was a man of courage, unafraid of the political powers or the religious elite (14:3-4; Luke 3:7-8). John was sent to prepare the way for the coming of the Savior. Under the Law of Moses, the priests sacrificed the lambs. God chose the son of a priest (Luke 1:5-9) to introduce the Lamb of God to the world. John introduced Jesus to Andrew and one other person, possibly John the apostle – the same man who recorded the story we read in John 1. He even recorded the very hour of the day in which he went home with Jesus (John 1:39). He would never forget the day he beheld the Lamb of God.

Not only did God choose the son of a priest to introduce Jesus to the world, but the priests of Jerusalem would also play a vital role in the sacrifice of the Lamb of God. The chief priests delivered Jesus to Pilate, stood nearby accusing Him and inciting the people to cry, "Crucify Him!" (Luke 23:1-4, 10; Mark 14:1; 15:11). The high priest Caiaphas even said of Jesus, "[I]t is expedient for us that one man should die for the people" (John 11:50). He unwittingly spoke truth. The Jewish leaders did not enter the house of Pilate when they delivered Jesus to him because they wanted to remain ceremonially clean for the Passover (18:28), but they made themselves unclean by killing the Son of God!

The Jews gathered in Jerusalem to observe the feast of Passover that God had instituted 1,500 years before. The priests presented a pure and spotless Lamb for sacrifice. Peter said that we "were not redeemed with corruptible things, like silver or gold, from your aimless conduct received by tradition from your fathers, but with the precious blood of Christ, as of a lamb without blemish and without spot" (1 Peter 1:18-19; cf. Hebrews 4:15). The blood of Christ spilled from the altar of the cross to pay the debt for our sins.

The Day of Atonement has great relevance for the Christian. As a "shadow of the good things to come" (Hebrews 10:1), it paints a beautiful picture of Christ. Gordon Wenham notes, "For Hebrews [the book], the day of atonement prefigures the crucifixion. Christ on the cross achieved what the high priests of the Old Covenant had attempted to do on the day of atonement." [2]

• *He Is the High Priest.* Christ was not actually sacrificed by the priests. As the true High Priest and the Good Shepherd, He offered Himself freely for our sins (John 10:15). The high priest of the Day of Atonement was the one mediator between God and man who entered alone into the Most Holy Place on behalf of the people; Christ is now the great High Priest who is the mediator between God and man (1 Timothy 2:5; Hebrews 2:17; 3:1). Just as the high priest would enter through the veil once a year on the Day of Atonement to sprinkle the blood of the lamb on the ark of the covenant, so Christ has entered through the veil of heaven (4:12-16; 9:11). He is a greater High Priest than Aaron. Christ was sinless, so He did not have to offer a sacrifice for Himself before offering a sacrifice for the people (4:15; 5:3; 7:26-27).

• *He Is the Sacrifice.* Jesus is not only the High Priest; He is also the unblemished sacrifice (Hebrews 7:27; 9:14). His blood was sprinkled in the Most Holy Place (v. 12). On the Day of Atonement the carcass of the sin offering was burned outside the camp. Hebrews 13:11-12 applies this to Christ, who suffered outside the city gate of Jerusalem. Christ's sacrifice was greater than the levitical sacrifices because it was not repeated year after year but made once for all time (9:12).

Jesus' death gave humanity access to God that it never had been able to enjoy. Steve Stanley summarizes by saying, "The importance of coming into God's presence was illustrated by the high priest's entry into the holy of holies on behalf of the people, which was the cultic high point of the year. But as it was, the people had to be satisfied with a superficial and temporary cleansing that did not afford them direct and intimate access to God." [3] The veil of the temple was torn in two at the death of Jesus (Matthew 27:51; Mark 15:38; Luke 23:45), symbolizing that Jesus gave humanity access to God previously available only to the high priest. The child of God can now "hav[e] boldness to enter the Holiest by the blood of Jesus" (Hebrews 10:19). In the last chapter, we noted that God and sin do not mix just as oil and water do not mix. A doctor friend reminded me that soap causes oil and water to mix and that is how we can clean things. The blood of Jesus is the cleansing agent which makes it possible for us to be purified and united to God.

• *He Is the Difference.* Hebrews 10:4 presents a dilemma: "For it is not possible that the blood of bulls and goats could take away sins." In Leviticus 4:26 the Israelites were told they would be forgiven, and in 16:30 they were told, "You may be clean from all your sins before the Lord." The writer of Hebrews states that animals cannot cleanse sins, yet the children of Israel were told they were cleansed of their sins. How can both statements be true?

The author of the letter to the Hebrews was focusing on the temporary nature of the Levitical sacrifices as opposed to the permanent nature of the sacrifice of Christ. There is no evidence in the Old or New Testaments that sins were piled up or rolled forward. Rather, the text says there was a yearly "reminder" of sin because humanity's persistent sin required continual atonement (Hebrews 10:3). There were also built-in weaknesses to the Levitical system. An imperfect high priest offered an unwilling animal to take the place of a human being. Those sacrifices still resulted in forgiveness. How? Through the death of Christ. Forgiveness was based on the people's obedience and the certainty of Christ's coming and death.

There is no power in the water a person is baptized in, but salvation takes place at that point. How? Through the death of Christ (1 Peter 3:21). The sacrificial system looked forward to the cross just as the baptism of John did. Baptism in the name of Jesus Christ (Acts 2:38) looks back to the cross. It is true that the blood of bulls cannot forgive sin, and it is equally true that sins were forgiven in the Old Testament.[4] Jesus is the difference. He finally did for us what the blood of lambs could not do and what we could not do for ourselves. He is the perfect High Priest and sacrificial Lamb who willingly offered Himself as the one great sacrifice for all time (Hebrews 10:1-18). John

Hartley is correct in asserting, "Jesus' death has thus accomplished the full intent of both the Day of Atonement and the whole sacrificial system."[5] No more lambs need to die, for the Lamb of God has taken away the sins of the world!

Conclusion

The imagery of the Lamb is significant in the New Testament. It emphasizes the connection between the sacrificial system of the Old Testament and the sacrifice of Christ. The Lamb of God has now become the Shepherd of God's sheep (John 10). He wants to save us and protect us. In the Highlands of Scotland, a sheep will often wander off where the grass is very sweet. The sheep will jump down 10 or 12 feet to get to it. But then it cannot jump back up, and the shepherd can hear it bleating in distress. A sheep may be there for days or until it has eaten all the grass. The shepherd will wait until the sheep is so faint it cannot stand, and then he will put a rope around himself and go down and pull the sheep back up to safety.

The shepherd must wait a long time because if he goes down to get the sheep before it is totally exhausted, fear and excitement will cause the sheep to jump off the cliff. The shepherd must wait until the sheep is so tired it will let the shepherd lift it up.[6] Are we willing to stop trying to find happiness and salvation by our own means? Are we ready to let the Good Shepherd have control of our lives? Do you want to be delivered from the angel of death? Then watch the Lamb and trust the Shepherd!

Discussion Questions

1. What would you have been thinking if you were in little Ethan's shoes on the night the death angel came?

2. Would you be able to cut a lamb's throat for your sins? How should this affect the way we view what Jesus did for us?

3. Have you been taught previously that Old Testament sins were "rolled forward"? Has this chapter changed your view of this?

Looking Ahead

What lessons did you learn from the events of Sept. 11, 2001?

Section 3:
Forgiveness Seized

Chapter 9

The Greatest Tragedy

I remember listening to Woodrow Stewart, a deacon of the Lord's church in Elizabethtown, Ky., talk about being at Pearl Harbor on Dec. 7, 1941. My parents, Joe and Dorothy Brothers, remember exactly where they were when they heard about the assassination of John F. Kennedy on Nov. 22, 1963. My dad said he was in a sociology class at the University of Tennessee Martin. At 1 p.m. his professor came into the classroom, announced that the president was dead and dismissed class. I will never forget what I was doing on Tuesday, Sept. 11, 2001, when I heard about the World Trade Center attacks. My guess is that you will never forget either. The images of that day are forever etched on the monument of our memories. From that time forward, our nation, the world and the church have searched for what to do next.

It is sobering to reflect on events like Pearl Harbor, the Oklahoma City bombing or Sept. 11, 2001, and then to focus on the subject of forgiveness. Events like these may serve to give us greater insight into what forgiveness is and how much God loves us. One passage where the tragedies of the past may help us is Colossians 1:14: "[I]n whom we have redemption through His blood, the forgiveness of sins." In our last lesson we focused on atonement; in this lesson we move our attention to redemption. This chapter moves us from forgiveness shown to forgiveness seized.

Reviewing Colossians

The city of Colosse lay 100 miles east of Ephesus. Epaphras established the church there (Colossians 1:7), and he was with Paul at the writing of the letter to the Colossian brethren. Epaphras may have brought Paul news of a false teaching affecting the congregations in the area of the Lycus Valley (where Colosse was located). This false teaching is known today as the "Colossian heresy." One must glean the nature of this teaching from the content of the Colossian letter (cf. also Ephesians). This process is much like determining the content of a telephone conversation by listening to only one side of the conversation.[1] Thomas Schreiner notes, "Scholars have made 44 different identifications of the opponents in Colossae."[2] Because of that, it is difficult to pinpoint the exact teaching and its source, but one can glean enough information from the text to get an adequate picture of the problem. Some of the elements include:

1. It was a mixture of Jewish, pagan and Christian elements.

2. Emphasis was placed on the hierarchies of the spiritual powers of the universe with special attention to (and possibly worship of) angels (Colossians 2:18-19).

3. Christ's supremacy and the completeness of His scheme of redemption were undermined (1:15-19).

4. Emphasis was placed on what was probably Hellenistic philosophy (2:8).

5. Jewish traditions were bound on Christians (2:16).

6. Asceticism seems to have been part of it as well (2:21-23).[3]

Paul wrote the Colossian letter to address this situation. He elaborated on the person and work of Christ. He stressed Christ's superiority over the principalities and powers the heresy promoted. He showed the intimate connection between Jesus and His people ("His body"). In light of this connection, there was no need for Christians to pay homage to forces over which Christ reigned supreme.[4]

Redemption's True Meaning

The important element of this review is that the heresy was focused on Jesus Christ. In addressing this problem, Paul gives us insight into what our Savior has done for us.

My guess is that most of us do not like the feeling of being trapped. A Japanese war plane dropped an 1,760 pound bomb, which struck just forward of turret gun number two on the starboard side of the USS Arizona at 8:10 a.m. on Dec. 11, 1941. The ensuing explosion tore the front part of the ship apart and sent her to the bottom of Pearl Harbor. Sadly, 1,177 crewman died with her. Many of them were trapped inside the ship as it rapidly descended.[5] The thought of their final moments puts a lump in my throat and a heaviness in my heart.

Similarly, we are all trapped in sin. Paul tells us that "all have sinned and fall short of the glory of God" (Romans 3:23). We are slaves to sin, trapped by Satan and separated from the God we love (Isaiah 59:1-2). As sinners we live "having no hope and without God in the world" (Ephesians 2:12).

Countless firemen and policemen flooded into the World Trade Center as others tried desperately to get out. In trying to save the lives of others, 343 fire and police personnel died. Through these deaths we get a glimpse of what our Savior did to free us. Just as many people sacrificed themselves to save others in the tragedy of Sept. 11, 2001, our Savior sacrificed Himself to save the world from the worst terrorist of all time – Satan.

Paul stated of Jesus, "[I]n whom we have redemption" (Colossians 1:14). We did not discuss the idea of redemption in our study of Old Testament terms, but it has a rich Old Testament heritage (*ga'al* in Leviticus 27:15; *padah* in Psalm 31:5).[6] Jack Cottrell, in his book *God the Redeemer*, defined redemption as "the idea of rescuing or setting free by paying some kind of price." The word *go'el*, the participle form for the verb *ga'al*, was the term used to describe the "kinsman redeemer" in the Old Testament. This person was the near-relative who was responsible for redeeming family members who had sold themselves into slavery or had sold their family land because of debt. The kinsman redeemer also restored justice to those who were unable to provide it for themselves. Boaz played the role of kinsman redeemer for Ruth. *Go'el* is used "extensively in the Old Testament to refer to God's redemptive work." God is our kinsman redeemer.[7]

The word "redemption" in Colossians 1:14 derives from the Greek term, *apolutrosis* (a-po-**loo**-tro-sis), which means "a releasing effected by payment of ransom." [8] N.T. Wright notes that this word "as used in the ancient world in general, is from a root which carried the meaning (capable of metaphorical use) of 'purchase from the slave-market.' " [9] It emphasizes two things: release and ransom. We are released from the power of Satan and sin, but this release comes only with a ransom. The ransom paid for our freedom from sin was the blood of Jesus Christ (1 Peter 1:18-19).

Remission of Sins

"Forgiveness" in Colossians 1:14 is the Greek word *aphesis*. You may recall from our discussion in chapter 6 that this word means "pardon of sins (letting them go as if they had never been committed), remission (forgiveness) of the penalty." [10] Remission/forgiveness stress that we have been pardoned from the punishment we deserve. Redemption stresses that we were set free from what imprisoned us. We are not only like those trapped in the World Trade Center; we are also like the terrorists. We are sinners who have attacked God. We are His enemies (Ephesians 2:15-16), so we deserve God's wrath. However, He chose to punish His son instead of punishing us (Isaiah 53:6-7). Jesus paid the price for us, making peace between us and God (Colossians 1:20-22). Christ was treated as if He was us, so we could be treated as if we were Him.

Imagine that it is 9:03 a.m. on April 19, 1995, and you have just dropped off your preschooler at the day care in the Murrah Federal Building in Downtown Oklahoma City. A sudden explosion rocks the landscape and you turn around to find smoke and rubble where you just left your child. Timothy McVeigh was executed on July 11, 2001, for setting off the bomb that resulted in the deaths of 168 people. If your child had been one of the 19 children killed by McVeigh's ruthless act, how would you feel about him? Would you have been willing to take his place on death row? Would you have been willing to adopt him into your family? Does that sound ludicrous to you? That is exactly what God and Christ have done for all of us. That is what Paul, a former terrorist himself, was saying of Christ, "[I]n whom we have redemption through His blood, the forgiveness of sins" (Colossians 1:14).

Responding to the Gift

How can we respond to such a selfless act and such a precious gift? Simply put, we accept the gift. Imagine a person who has just been freed from the rubble of the World Trade Center saying to the man who risked his life to rescue him or her, "Thanks, but no thanks. I don't want to be saved," and then crawling back into the rubble. Unbelievable! Yet, that is what many people do to God. Our Father has offered us freedom from sin. Paul tells us in Romans 6 that at our baptism we re-enact the death, burial and resurrection of Jesus and are freed from our sins (vv. 3-8; see also Colossians 1:12-14). Unfortunately, many listen to invitation after invitation and fail to respond. They are saying to God, "Thanks, but no thanks. I don't want your help. Leave me here in sin." Unimaginable!

Responding to God's love is just like falling in love. My wife, Cindy, and I met at a Christian college at the beginning of our sophomore year. We married a little less than four years later. Several things had to happen before that took place: we decided that we loved each other (she was dating someone else when I decided); we then voiced that love to each other. Do you think she would have stayed with me if I had told her, "I love you but I am a little embarrassed about it. Would you mind if we didn't tell anyone else?" If my love was true, I wouldn't mind others knowing about it. The next thing we did was stop dating other people. If I told her that I loved her on Monday and then went out with someone else every other night of the week, she would not have put up with me. She needed to know that she was the only one for me. At some point we made a lifelong commitment to share our love and lives. Ultimately, at a wedding ceremony, we publically proclaimed our love for one another and made a permanent pledge to each other. Only after that could we become husband and wife and enjoy all the blessings of married life. We were not one in God's eyes until the moment of our marriage.

Our relationship with God is the same. We must decide that we believe in Him (Hebrews 11:6; John 20:30-31). We must be willing to confess that belief before our fellow human beings (Romans 10:9-10). If we are ashamed for others to know that we believe, then God will be ashamed of us (Matthew 10:32; Luke 9:26). Next, we must stop "dating" the devil; we must repent or turn away from our old life of sin and commit ourselves totally to God alone (Luke 13:3; Acts 17:30; 26:20).

After all that, we are still not one with God until we participate in the wedding ceremony of baptism. Only at baptism are our sins washed away, and we are added to the saved (Acts 2:38-41, 47; 22:16). Baptism makes us part of His body (1 Corinthians 12:13), which is the church (Ephesians 1:22-23), and His bride (5:22-33). Just as we say "I do" at a wedding ceremony, so we say "I do" before our baptism when we are asked, "Do you believe that Jesus Christ is the Son of the living God?" (Acts 8:37). Just as we put on wedding clothes at a wedding ceremony, so we are clothed with Christ at the moment of our baptism (Galatians 3:26-27). He cleanses us in baptism so He might present us to Himself (Ephesians 5:26-27). To claim "oneness" with God without being baptized is like living with someone without getting married. Are you one with God? Have you accepted the gift?

After baptism, we must devote the new life we have been given to the service of God (Romans 12:1-2). In a speech delivered on the day of the terrorist tragedy, President Bush said, "None of us will ever forget this day, yet we go forward to defend freedom and all that is good and just in our world." As Christians we must devote our lives to what is "good and just." Paul describes this in Romans 6:11-13:

> Likewise you also, reckon yourselves to be dead indeed to sin, but alive to God in Christ Jesus our Lord. Therefore do not let sin reign in your mortal body, that you should obey it in its lusts. And do not present your members as instruments of unrighteousness to sin, but present yourselves to God as being alive from the dead, and your members as instruments of righteousness to God.

God gives us new spiritual lives when we express our faith in baptism. He then calls on us to devote our new lives to His purposes as a "living sacrifice" (12:1-8). Conversion must be followed by commitment. Transition must be followed by transformation.

Conclusion

Dan McWilliams was traveling from Ground Zero toward the Hudson river. He spotted a 3-by-5 flag flying on the deck of a boat and an idea popped into his mind. He picked up the flag, wrapped it around the broken pole, and started back toward Ground Zero. Along the way he met George Johnson, a member of his ladder company from Brooklyn, and invited him to help. Dan and George encountered Billy Eisengrein, who also joined them. Dan and Billy had known each other since they were young boys on Staten Island.

The three men arrived at Ground Zero and immediately found what they were looking for – a pole, likely from the remains of the Marriott hotel, was lifted up about 20 feet above the ground and leaning at a 45-degree angle. They began to raise the flag on that pole, unaware that about 100 feet to their west, under a pedestrian walkway, a reporter by the name of Thomas E. Franklin happened to be looking eastward, and we had a moment captured in time.[11] A picture was taken that would be seen around the world. It was a moment that would inspire a nation. This picture declared, "We will rise again. There is hope. We can overcome!"

Another picture was taken 2,000 years ago and captured in the pages of God's Word. It is not a picture of a flag raised on a pole by firemen but of a Savior being raised on a cross by Roman soldiers. The Word also shows the Savior being raised on a cloud back into heaven. These pictures shout down through the ages, "He did rise again. There is hope. We can overcome sin. Through Him we have been redeemed!" To forget the events of Sept. 11, 2001, would be a terrible tragedy. To read Colossians 1:14 and walk away unchanged would be the greatest tragedy.

Discussion Questions

1. What were you doing when you heard about the events of Sept. 11, 2001? How has it changed you?

2. Do you feel that the events of that day can help us to better understand what God has done for us?

3. What was your initial response when you read that we also are the terrorists? How could this affect your view of forgiveness?

Looking Ahead

Have you ever turned down a gift?

Chapter 10

Accepting the Gift

M y older daughter Katie was afraid of men for the first year of her life. That changed when we moved to Hatley, Miss., and she met Johnny Camp. She was 13 months old, and he was in his 70's. Mr. Johnny died a week after attending Katie's second birthday party. They loved each other more in one year than some people do in a lifetime. A picture of them together graces our bookshelf at home. I have a video of the last time Mr. Johnny came to visit Katie, a few days before he had a massive heart attack. In that video Mr. Johnny asked Katie, "How much do you love me." She dropped the basketball she was holding, spread out her arms as far as she could, and said, "Dis much." As I reflect on this scene, there is another scene of love that floods into my mind. It is set just outside ancient Jerusalem 2,000 years ago. There I can imagine the world saying, "How much to you love us?" I then see Jesus' arms spread on the cross of Calvary. He is saying, "I love you this much."

The last three chapters have focused on Jesus stretching forth His arms as peacemaker, sacrificial lamb and redeemer. Yet, the story is incomplete. Chapter 9 began to discuss what we do in response to Jesus' sacrifice, but we need to explore this further. In this lesson we will emphasize what we should do to accept the peace and the atoning sacrifice Jesus offers.

The Process of Acceptance

The first thing to consider is how we respond to Jesus as the peacemaker. Paul tells us "we have peace with God" (Romans 5:1), and he also tells us the peacemaker is Jesus Christ. But he does not stop there. He tells us the process by which we accept the terms of peace.

On April 9, 1865, Ulysses S. Grant jogged along the Virginia road that lead to Appomattox Court House. It was quiet, even for a Sunday. The mighty guns of war were silent. Two armies sat motionless on either side of the road … waiting. They awaited the outcome of a meeting in which the Southern commander, Robert E. Lee, was to surrender to Grant. Lee was stiff and cool as the meeting began. It was not easy to surrender. Union officers made attempts to ease the tension with small talk, but to no avail. When Grant began to speak, he did not speak of surrender or terms, but he spoke of the Mexican War in which they both had fought. It was Lee who finally had to bring up the business of the day. Grant silently wrote down the terms of surrender and handed them to his adversary. Lee wiped and adjusted his glasses and read the simple terms: the enlisted men were to surrender their arms, the officers to retain theirs, all were to be given their paroles and go home, not to be disturbed by United States authority so long as they kept their promise not to fight the government again.

Lee was pleasantly surprised. His icy exterior began to melt. This was much better than what the Southern politicians had told him to expect from the North. He was especially pleased that the officers could keep their weapons. "This will have a very happy effect upon my army," he said. Grant asked if Lee had anything more to suggest. Lee wondered if those in his army who owned their horses may keep them. Although it was not in the terms, Grant allowed it. He even went a step further and told his officers to allow each Southerner to claim a horse or mule to take home. They would need them to rebuild their farms. When Grant learned that the Confederate army was on the verge of starvation, he sent word through his army for every soldier who had three rations to turn over two to the Confederate army. Union troops cheered and fired their weapons at the surrender, but Grant stopped it, saying, "The rebels are our countrymen again: the best sign of rejoicing after the victory will be to abstain from all demonstrations on the field." [1]

The graciousness of General Grant illustrates how God has treated us. He has gone the extra mile for us. He did for us what He did not have to do, but there must be terms of surrender. What are those terms? How do we accept the peace God offers? Romans 5:1 teaches that we have peace with God if we have been "justified by faith." Is faith the key to accepting the peace of God? In Romans 3:24 Paul says we are "freely justified by His grace." Is God's grace the key? Does He just give me peace without any action on my part? Are we justified by grace or by faith? The Bible says both. Grace is the cause of justification, and faith is the means. God makes justification available to us, and faith is how we accept the gift. Paul makes it clear that salvation does not come through circumcision or the Old Law (Romans 3–4) or our good deeds (Titus 3:4-5). The terms of surrender are "by grace, through faith."

We cannot earn salvation or be righteous (Romans 3:10). None of us will ever be good enough to go to heaven on our own. Our actions can earn only the wage of death. Our hope lies in the conviction that if we will trust in God He will treat us as if we are righteous, and He will give us eternal life as a gift (Romans 6:23). We must notice the difference between the two ideas: you earn a wage, but you receive a gift because someone loves you. Salvation is a gift of love. Also, although salvation is a gift, there must be a point of acceptance. If someone offers you a gift, you can either reach out and accept it, or you can reject it. Faith is the means by which we reach out and accept the gift of God.

Is there a way of knowing when our faith has accepted the gift? Is there a time of exchange that we can point to? Paul tells us in Romans 6,

> [K]nowing this, that our old man was crucified with Him, that the body of sin might be done away with, that we should no longer be slaves of sin. For he who has died has been *freed* from sin. Now if we died with Christ, we believe that we shall also live with Him, knowing that Christ, having been raised from the dead, dies no more. Death no longer has dominion over Him" (vv. 6-8, emphasis mine).

The word translated as "freed" in verse 7 is the same word that is translated "justified" in Romans 5:1.[2] Paul says we are "justified" or "freed" from our sins when we die with Christ.

So when do we die with Christ? Look at Romans 6:2-4:

> How shall we who died to sin live any longer in it? Or do
> you not know that as many of us as were baptized into Christ
> Jesus were baptized into His death? Therefore we were
> buried with Him through baptism into death, that just as
> Christ was raised from the dead by the glory of the Father,
> even so we also should walk in newness of life.

We die with Christ at our baptism. Baptism expresses our faith and tells
God we want the gift. God extends the gift to us through the death, burial and resurrection of Jesus; we accept the gift through re-enacting the
death, burial and resurrection of Jesus at our baptism.

The Difference Between Faith and Works

Some struggle with the idea that baptism could be the point at which
sins are forgiven. They point to Paul's statement to the Ephesian brethren
that they were saved through grace, "not of works, lest anyone should
boast" (Ephesians 2:8-9). These doubters would classify baptism as a
work that cannot be connected with salvation. But Paul did not classify every human action as a work. Repentance and confession are human works, yet each is necessary in order to be saved (Luke 13:3; Acts
2:38; Romans 10:9-10). Most who reject the connection between baptism and salvation would readily accept the connection between repentance and salvation. Very few actually believe that no human actions are connected with salvation. Some have chosen to put baptism
into a separate category from repentance and confession. This is due
largely to the influence of the reformation leader Ulrich Zwingli of
Zurich, Switzerland (1448-1531), a contemporary of Martin Luther
and John Calvin. Before Zwingli began teaching otherwise, almost
unanimous agreement existed in the Christian world (including Luther)
that baptism was the point at which sins were forgiven.[3] If one labels
baptism as a human work, he should be consistent and do the same with
repentance and confession. Baptism does not earn salvation, but Romans
6 makes it clear that baptism is the point at which we are justified.

Paul stated, "For by grace you have been saved through faith, and
that not of yourselves; it is the gift of God, not of works, lest anyone
should boast" (Ephesians 2:8-9). Was Paul really teaching that baptism

was unnecessary for salvation? Describing the process of salvation in verses 4-6 he stated, "But God, who is rich in mercy, because of His great love with which He loved us, even when we were dead in trespasses, made us alive together with Christ (by grace you have been saved), and raised us up together, and made us sit together in the heavenly places in Christ Jesus." How does God save us by grace? He makes us alive and raises us with Christ even while we are dead in our sins. When does God's grace make us alive with Christ?

> [We are] buried with Him in baptism, in which you also were raised with Him through faith in the working of God, who raised Him from the dead. And you, being dead in your trespasses and the uncircumcision of your flesh, He has made alive together with Him, having forgiven you all trespasses (Colossians 2:12-13).

What did Paul mean when he said that God by grace through faith made us alive and raised us up with Christ? Our baptism! What was Paul talking about when he said that we were "justified by faith"? Our baptism!

This does not mean that we earn our salvation at baptism. We are merely complying with the God-appointed terms of acceptance. Imagine a man is drowning, and a ship comes to his aid. A crew member tosses the drowning man a life preserver. The man grabs it and is pulled to safety. Did he save himself? Of course not. Someone else tossed the preserver and pulled him to safety. But had he not grabbed it he would have died. All we are doing in baptism is grabbing the life preserver.

Created for Works, Justified by Faith

Paul notes in Ephesians 2:10 that "we are His workmanship, created in Christ Jesus for good works, which God prepared beforehand that we should walk in them." The purpose of our Christian life is good works. They are necessary in order to please God, and Paul repeatedly emphasized obedience in the letter to the Romans (1:5; 5:19; 6:16; 15:18; 16:19, 26). James 2:24 also states, "You see then that a man is justified by works, and not by faith only." How can a person be justified by faith (Romans 5:1) *and* by works (James 2:24)? The difference is the contrast between "cause" and "means." The Word of God says works are not the *cause* of salvation (Ephesians 2:9). No one can be truly righteous; we can never pile up enough good works to deserve heaven. When works are viewed as the *means* of expressing one's faith and accepting the gift of salvation, the Word says, "not by faith alone" (James 2:24). J.D. Thomas states, "The sort of work in each case might be exactly the same, but the motivation and the principle upon which it is done is different in the two systems." [4] One system requires perfection and leads to arrogance, and the other requires faithfulness and leads to humility.

The Pattern of the New Testament

The second consideration is how we respond to Jesus as the Lamb. We realize that we are sinners in need of help. We recognize that Jesus was sacrificed as the Passover Lamb for our sins. The blood of the Savior is the anti-venom for the poison of sin. But now we seek to find out what we, the sinners, must do. Do we automatically have forgiveness? Do we automatically go to heaven? What do we do? Watch the Lamb!

Acts 8 tells of a man who had questions. He was 1,000 miles from home. Ethiopia lay along the Nile river, south of Egypt. [5] A man of power and wealth, the Ethiopian eunuch rode along in his chariot with the joy of worship in Jerusalem burning brightly in his heart. His wealth as treasurer for the queen of his nation afforded him the privilege of owning a scroll of the prophet Isaiah. He passed the hours on the journey home by reading from the powerful message of this great prophet. No doubt his brow furrowed as he struggled to understand the meaning of the words. There was no one to assist him in his understanding and little chance that someone in his homeland would be able to help. Suddenly a man appeared in the road and asked him if he understood what he was reading. The eunuch was no doubt startled at first, but he likely was intrigued by Philip's question. He answered, "How can I, unless someone guides me?" (Acts 8:31). He invited Philip into the chariot and read to him: "He was led as a sheep to the slaughter; And as a lamb before its shearer is silent, So He opened not His mouth. In His humiliation His justice was taken away, And who will declare His generation? For His life is taken from the earth" (vv. 32-33; Isaiah 53:7-8). The eunuch then asked, "[O]f whom does the prophet say this, of himself or of some other man?" (Acts 8:34). Philip began at the quot- ed scripture and "preached Jesus to him" (v. 35).

Does the passage from Isaiah 53 sound familiar? We discussed it in chapter 8 as a prophecy of the coming Lamb of God. If we watch how the eunuch responded to the sacrifice of the Lamb of God, then we can learn what we should do. Acts 8 says that the eunuch believed, confessed his faith, and was baptized for the forgiveness of his sins. We find this same pattern of response throughout the book of Acts (2:38; 8:12; 9:18; 10:48), and it is supported throughout the New Testament (Romans 6:3; 1 Peter 3:21). The text of Acts 8 also reveals that the eunuch rejoiced after his conversion as he continued his jour- ney home (v. 39). So should we.

How have we responded to the sacrifice of the Lamb? Have we gazed on the spilled blood of Jesus and walked away unmoved? Have we lis- tened to numerous invitations and failed to express our faith in re- pentance, confession and baptism? Have some of us become Christians and then "crucified again" the Son of God by going back to our old lives of sin (cf. Hebrews 6:6)? Do we need to confess our sins so that the blood of the Lamb may continue to cleanse us (1 John 1:7-9)? Have we lost the joy and excitement the eunuch felt? Has Christianity be- come just a routine we go through?

Isn't it time we found the joy of living with the Lamb? Whether one focuses on Jesus as peacemaker, sacrifice or redeemer, a remarkable picture of consistency is painted in the Bible of how we are to respond to and accept His offer of forgiveness.

Conclusion

Once upon a time, there was a man whose duty was to raise a draw- bridge to allow boats to pass on a river below and then to lower it for the trains to cross the river. One day this man's son came to work with him to watch. Curious as most boys are apt to be, he peeked into a trap- door that was always left open so his father could keep an eye on the machinery that controlled the bridge. Suddenly, the boy lost his foot- ing and tumbled into the gears. As the father reached to pull his son out, he heard the whistle of an approaching train. He knew that the train would be full of people and impossible to stop. The bridge must be lowered. But what of his son? He faced a terrible dilemma. He did not have time to save his son and lower the bridge. Whom would he choose? He tried frantically to free the boy but could not. He was running out of time. Countless people would die. With tears streaming down his face, he reached out and pulled the lever that controlled the lowering of the bridge. The bridge fell into place just in time to save the passengers on the train. The father gazed on the passengers as they rumbled past. They were laughing and enjoying their trip, oblivious of what the father had just done for them.[6] Our heavenly Father gave up His Son for us. Will we ride by and ignore His sacrifice?

Discussion Questions

1. What kind of response do you want to see from people when you give them a gift? Want kind of response does God want from us?

2. Is baptism a work of God or a work of man? Does God do something to save us at baptism or are we saving ourselves?

3. How do you think God feels when we reject the gift of His Son?

Looking Ahead

Why is it hard to forgive others?

Section 4:
Forgiveness Seen

Chapter 11

The Fragrance of Christ

W e now make a transition from forgiveness seized to forgiveness seen, learning about the transformation that should take place in our lives after we seize the forgiveness God has shown through Christ. We will explore the change in attitude and action that should be seen in those forgiven by the grace of God. Mark Twain once said, "Forgiveness is the fragrance that the flower leaves on the heel of the one who crushed it." [1] Paul says that this fragrance should be in the life of every Christian: "And be kind to one another, tenderhearted, forgiving one another, even as God in Christ forgave you" (Ephesians 4:32). That is easier said than done. When you feel the pain of another's boot, the last thing you want to do is forgive. How do you put the hurt aside? How do you swallow your pride? The answer is Jesus. In Matthew 18 we can see what Jesus teaches us about showing forgiveness.

Seven Times

Do you have someone who has caused you great pain and anguish? Is it hard to think of him without becoming upset? Does he say he is sorry then turn around and hurt you again? Do you find yourself saying, "How long do I have to go on forgiving this person? He doesn't care about me. How much is enough?" If you answered any of these questions with a "yes," then you may know how Peter was feeling when he spoke to Jesus in Matthew 18:21-22: "Then Peter came to Him and said, 'Lord, how often shall my brother sin against me, and I forgive him? Up to seven times?' Jesus said to him, 'I do not say to you, up to seven times, but up to seventy times seven.' "

Peter's question was likely prompted by an earlier discussion. Matthew 18:15-20 records Jesus' teaching concerning how God's people should respond to a brother or sister caught in sin. Jesus gives them a procedure to follow when handling such issues and challenges them to keep the issue as small as possible. Approach the offender in private initially. If that fails, take a couple of others with you to encourage the erring brother or sister and to serve as witnesses to the discussion. Only when all of this has failed do you go to the church. It is all to be handled within the church.

The discussion of the church's response to an erring member may have prompted Peter to wonder to what extent he was expected to forgive. Peter did not just pick the number seven out of the air. Some scholars say that the rabbis taught to forgive someone seven times.[2] The number seven is commonly associated with perfection or completeness in the Hebrew mind-set. Other scholars would say that the rabbis only required that you forgive a person three times.[3] Either way, Peter was not asking for less than the rabbis asked and may well have been willing to do more. Jesus said that we are to forgive as many times as "seventy times seven." He was not saying we should have a sheet on the refrigerator door and mark off each time we forgive someone until we reach 490 times. The message is to keep on forgiving. Go far beyond what human beings think is enough. Forgiveness is to be a way of life. We are to forgive as many times as necessary.

Story Details

Parables make up approximately 75 percent of Jesus' recorded teaching and 52 percent of the book of Luke.[4] To drive His point home to Peter, Jesus told a parable of a king settling accounts with his servants (Matthew 18:23-35). One servant owed the king 10,000 talents (one talent equaled 6,000 denarii). One denarius was a day's wage for unskilled labor. The servant would have had to work 60,000,000 days to pay off his debt.[5] He begged to have his debt forgiven, and his request was granted. The servant was forgiven a debt that he could not possibly have paid. One would think he would be so moved with gratitude that he would want to show the same kindness to others.

Such was not the case. Instead, the servant found a fellow servant who only owed him 100 denarii. This debt could be paid off in 100 days (about four months). The ratio between what the two servants owed was 600,000 to 1. The forgiven servant would not forgive the small debt of his fellow servant and had him cast into debtor's prison. When the other servants saw this, they made it known to the king. The king cast the first servant into prison for failing to show the same kindness he had received. As Peter reflected on the fate of the unmerciful servant, it probably made 70 times seven look more attractive.

Self Application

A couple who had been married for 15 years began having more disagreements than usual. They wanted their marriage to work, so they agreed on an idea the wife had. For one month they would drop a slip into a "fault" box any time they were irritated by something the other did. They sat down to dinner at the end of the month and opened their boxes. The husband went first and read one by one his wife's frustrations with him: "Left the top off of the jelly jar; wet towels on the shower floor; dirty socks not in the hamper"; the list went on. The husband reflected on what he had done wrong while his wife opened her box and began reading. Every single piece of paper in her box said the same thing: "I love you!" [6]

Many of us spend our lives focusing on what others have done to hurt us. That was the attitude of Peter and the unmerciful servant. The parable of the unmerciful servant challenged Peter to consider how God treats us. The Father could make a long list of the things we have done to hurt Him, but the message He sends over and over is "I love you!" Just as the kindness of the master should have inspired the servant to show mercy to his fellow servant, so the kindness of God should inspire us to forgive one another. This teaching also instructs us in what our attitude should be when practicing church discipline (Matthew 18:15-20).

It is not enough to consider the message that Jesus was giving to Peter; we must apply it to ourselves. We are called to forgive as God forgave: "And be kind to one another, tenderhearted, forgiving one another, even as God in Christ forgave you" (Ephesians 4:32). Paul stressed this action to Titus. Titus was instructed to challenge the Cretan brethren "to be peaceable, gentle, showing all humility to all men" (Titus 3:2). No doubt the Cretan brethren struggled with this teaching because the people of Crete were "liars, evil beasts, lazy gluttons" (1:12). How could they be "peaceable" with such people? Paul reminded Titus that they were once "foolish, disobedient, deceived, serving various lusts and pleasures, living in malice and envy, hateful and hating one another" (3:3). He went on to say that God in kindness and love showed them mercy anyway (vv. 4-7). The Cretan brethren were treated better than they deserved, and they were expected to treat their neighbors in kind. Paul was speaking to us as well. We have been treated better than we deserved, and we are therefore to "be kind to one another, tenderhearted, forgiving one another, even as God in Christ forgave you." Jesus said the same to Peter.

A direct link exists between how we treat others and how God treats us: "So My heavenly Father also will do to you if each of you, from his heart, does not forgive his brother his trespasses" (Matthew 18:35; cf. 6:12, 14-15). A direct link is also between how we treat others and how others treat us. We often want people to overlook our faults, but we are unwilling to overlook theirs. When we fail to show mercy to others, the "fellow servants" often take note of it. They notice it and treat us accordingly. Forgiveness blesses both the giver and the receiver. The receiver has the burden of guilt lifted. The giver has the burden of bitterness lifted, and he will be treated more compassionately by God and others. Agnes Sanford stated, "As we practice the work of forgiveness we discover more and more that forgiveness and healing are one." [7]

God not only forgives sin, but He also forgets it (Jeremiah 31:34). If we are to be as perfect as our heavenly Father (Matthew 5:48), then we must do the same for each other. We cannot simply wipe it from our memory banks, but we can choose not to dwell on it or speak of it. Some believe you can walk alongside of sin; in other words, you forgive, but you do not forget. Others say that they have forgiven someone, but they remind the other person every chance they get. Such attitudes are totally foreign to God's message. God forgets our sin. It is removed "as far as the east is from the west" (Psalm 103:12). If another person repents, then we must forgive. We should not bury the hatchet with the handle sticking out so we can grab it anytime we wish. If we forgive someone, we cannot bring the error up again. Forgiveness means that the sin no longer exists. Jesus' parable in Matthew 18 teaches that God treats us as we treat others. If we walk beside the sins of others, God will walk beside our sins instead of removing them. If He does, we are lost. Thomas Adams noted, "He that demands mercy, and shows none, ruins the bridge over which he himself is to pass." [8]

Savior's Example

We have learned that we were made for relationship and representation. Humanity repeatedly rejected this divine purpose. Therefore, Jesus, the exact image of God (Colossians 1:15), came to us as God's representative to repair the broken relationship between God and man and to show us how people who are God's representatives are supposed to live. Jesus' statement in John 13:15 is an apt description of His life: "For I have given you an example, that you should do as I have done to you." Jesus not only told us about the heart of God, He showed us. He also showed us how we were meant to be.

Jesus taught us to forgive and then showed us how to do it. Peter saw the lesson Jesus taught in Matthew 18 lived out on the cross of Calvary: "And when they had come to the place called Calvary, there they crucified Him, and the criminals, one on the right hand and the other on the left. Then Jesus said, 'Father, forgive them, for they do not know what they do'" (Luke 23:33-34). In the aftermath of the cross and his own denial of Christ, Peter experienced Christ's forgiveness along the shores of Galilee when Jesus commanded him, "Feed My sheep" (John 21:15-17). Despite Peter's denial, Jesus loved him, forgave him and put him to work in His kingdom. As the flower leaves its fragrance on the boot that crushes it, so Christ left the fragrance of forgiveness on Peter's heart. It can be found on our hearts as well!

I once was asked, "Can I keep asking God's forgiveness for the sin that I continue in, even when I think I try to stop doing it?" We all have certain sins that we struggle with more than others. Many people feel that God tires of listening to them ask for forgiveness. They struggle with feeling forgiven. Remember that Jesus told Peter to forgive someone who had sinned against him "seventy times seven" (Matthew 18:22). Would Jesus ask us to do something that He was not willing to practice Himself? He practiced what He preached. We must be sincere when we seek His forgiveness (2 Corinthians 7:10). We must also endeavor to change the wrong in our lives (Matthew 3:8; 1 Corinthians 6:9-11). If we keep asking sincerely and trying sincerely to change, then He keeps forgiving.

A Reminder

We are now at a point in our study where it might be helpful to summarize what we have learned about forgiveness. Forgiveness is the resumption of a broken relationship made possible because the crime that fractured the relationship has been removed. In other words, forgiveness is made possible because the offended chooses to treat the offender with kindness instead of the anger that he or she deserves. The offender must be willing to repent, and the offended must be willing to ransom (pay for, be punished for), remove (wash away, cleanse, blot out), and/or release (from the bondage of) the crime that fractured the relationship.

In the spiritual sense, this renewed relationship makes eternal salvation possible, should inspire holy living, and should lead to forgiveness of others by the one forgiven. In other words, if a person who has offended us is willing to repent, we are to forgive him. We should resume the relationship as if nothing had ever happened. If I am the person who was forgiven, then I should express gratitude to the one who has forgiven me and show the same attitude toward those who sin against me. God will then treat me as I have treated others.

Conclusion

A Spanish father and his son had become estranged. The son ran away, and the father set out to find him. He searched for months with no success. Finally, in a last desperate attempt, the father put an ad in a Madrid newspaper. It read: "Dear Paco, Meet me in front of this newspaper office at noon on Saturday. All is forgiven. I love you. Your Father." On Saturday, 800 Pacos showed up, looking for forgiveness and love from their fathers.[9] All about us are people who have felt the boot heel of a cruel world and their own sins. They are crushed and broken. They are seeking the fragrance of Christ. Will they see it in us?

Discussion Questions

1. How many times have you forgiven someone for the same offense?

2. Is there something for which others have had to forgive you repeatedly?

3. Why do you think we often want God to treat us better than we treat others?

Looking Ahead

If you died today, would you go to heaven?

Chapter 12

Digging Deeper

I spent two months living in Israel the summer after I graduated with my bachelor's degree. I spent one month of that time on an archaeological dig at the sight of the ancient city of Caesarea. My primary work was in Field G and Area 21 (dig sights are divided into squares that are given letter and number identifications). The job of my team was to confirm where the main street of Caesarea was when Paul, Cornelius and Philip lived there in the first century. Streets that had already been uncovered as well as a wall and towers on the Northern end of the city allowed us to make an educated guess as to the main street's location. To confirm this, we needed to dig deep into the sand of the Mediterranean coast. We discovered sidewalks, columns and paving stones which we felt confirmed the location of the road. Reflecting on this experience reminds me that sometimes we have to dig a little deeper to find the answers we are looking for. That is the purpose of this chapter. We have learned much in our study of forgiveness, but now it is time to dig a little deeper.

Confession of Our Sins

When seeking God's forgiveness, a human response is expected. Although Jesus asked the Father to forgive those who crucified Him (Luke 23:34), it does not mean they were forgiven and saved at that moment. Peter preached to many of those same people on the Day of Pentecost (Acts 2:36). Peter told them they must repent and be baptized "for the remission of sins" (v. 38). Jesus sought their forgiveness on the cross, but they did not receive it until they expressed their faith in repentance and baptism.

Sometimes we are asked if we must forgive those who will not repent. That is impossible to do. In Luke 17, Jesus said, "Take heed to yourselves. If your brother sins against you, rebuke him; and if he repents, forgive him. And if he sins against you seven times in a day, and seven times in a day returns to you, saying, 'I repent,' you shall forgive him" (vv. 3-4). Remember that forgiveness is about a broken relationship, and every relationship has two sides. One side must be willing to redeem, and the other must be willing to repent. If either fails, the relationship is not fully restored. They may remain in contact with each other, but there will always be a problem. We can offer forgiveness but they are not released of their guilt until they repent. So what do we do about people who do things to hurt us and do not ask for forgiveness?

First, we need to remember that an action is not necessarily a sin just because it hurts our feelings. Sin is a violation of God's law. Sometimes the problem with "we" is "me." Often, I need to get the chip off my shoulder and stop being so easily offended. The second thing we must remember is that if an action is sin, we have a responsibility to tell the offender about it (Luke 17:3; Galatians 6:1-2; Matthew 18:15). We spend far too much time talking *about* each other and far too little time talking *to* each other. Someone must be aware that he has sinned against us if he is to seek our forgiveness. I also think that there is such a thing as assumed or implied repentance. If the offender is someone who has a habit of trying to do right, would be sorry if he knew he had offended me, and has a daily habit of seeking God's forgiveness, then I often assume his repentance and forgive and forget. We must also remember that we are told to love everyone, whether they repent or not (5:44). In addition, we are not to feel bitterness toward others (Ephesians 4:31). Love and bitterness are separate issues from forgiveness (restoring the relationship, removing the penalty).

One of the best things we can do for a brother who has hurt us is pray that God will bless him (Matthew 5:44). It is hard to be angry with someone for whom you are regularly praying. If someone sins against us and has not repented, then we have to do one of two things: make him aware of the offense so he can repent or assume his repentance based on his life of walking in the light and forgive him. The same applies to us if we are the one who has done the offending. We need to go to the person we have sinned against and make it right (vv. 23-26).

We noted in chapter 10 that faith expressed in repentance, confession and baptism is the means by which humans contact the forgiveness of God. What about sins committed after baptism? Are we to be baptized again every time we sin? John gives us the answer: "If we confess our sins, He is faithful and just to forgive [*aphiemi*] us our sins and to cleanse us from all unrighteousness" (1 John 1:9). "To confess, used in connection with sins, means ... 'to say openly that one has sinned' 'to accuse oneself of one's own evil deeds.' " [1] John contrasts confession with claiming to have no sin in verse 10. The term translated "confess" in verse 9 is *homologeo*. This is the only passage in the New Testament in which this term is used in connection with sin (*exomologeo* is normally used – Matthew 3:6; James 5:16). *Homologeo* is usually used for confessing or acknowledging Jesus (Matthew 10:32; John 9:22; Romans 10:9; 1 John 2:23, 4:2, 15). By using this word, John is saying that we can choose to deny that we are sinners or we can acknowledge our sins to God. Only the latter are forgiven.

The question is often asked as to how public the confession should be. The adage "it should be as public as the sin" is a sound approach. If my sin is known by, sets a poor example for, or affects the congregation in some way, then I need to make it right before them. Otherwise, they will not know how to respond to me. The congregation has a responsibility to help lead me back from sin (Matthew 18:15ff; Galatians 6:1ff). Likewise, James says, "Confess your trespasses to one another, and pray for one another, that you may be healed. The effective, fervent prayer of a righteous man avails much" (5:16). We are reminded by James' words of the community nature of Christianity. We do not rejoice or gloat over each other's sins. We are to stand in the gap and intercede for one another as Moses interceded for Israel (Psalm 106:23).

Many think that fellow Christians will look down on them if they make a public confession of their sins. The church is not a museum where perfect specimens are put on display. It is more like a hospital where the spiritually sick are trying to get well by coming to the Great Physician. We suffer with the same afflictions and need each other. If others look down on you, that is their problem. We are responding to Jesus, not humans. Ultimately, His forgiveness is the forgiveness that matters most. He looks out for you but not down on you.

Pride is a hindrance to confession. It is no coincidence that in the same letter in which he enjoined us to confess sin, James also said, "God resists the proud, But gives grace to the humble" (James 4:6). David stated, "The sacrifices of God are a broken spirit, A broken and a contrite heart – These, O God, You will not despise" (Psalm 51:17). Vern McLellan adds, "Pride is the only disease that everyone around you suffers from except yourself." [2] For the proud, it is always someone else's fault. Consider the following:

> For example, we now blame someone else who we don't even know for making us smoke cigarettes … NASCAR fever causes us to drive fast, and society makes us commit crimes. We no longer take the blame for what we do ourselves, but at the drop of a hat, we will sue anyone in sight who we may blame for our own shortcomings.

> When our forefathers first came to this country, I wonder who they blamed for the first winters being cold and a shortage of food. If they had arrived in this country under today's standards, they would have sued the map maker for getting them off course, and the Native Americans would have been in trouble for providing them with food that could have caused them to increase their cholesterol intake. [3]

While it is true that we are enticed by things like beer commercials and cigarette ads, ultimately we are the ones responsible for our sins (James 1:14). We cannot blame God for our sins (v. 13); we cannot blame the devil, either. Each person is drawn away "by his own desires." Our sin is our fault! Confess it and conclude it.

Confidence in Our Salvation

A Christian might ask, "What if I sin and then die before I get a chance to repent?" Let me make two key statements before I seek to answer this question:

(1) There is a God, and I am not He. He will ultimately judge us and answer this question definitively.

(2) The best way to deal with this situation is to do everything in your power not to be in this situation.

Having made these disclaimers, let us see if there are some clues we can glean from the Bible.

Several questions must be considered. First of all, "What was the pattern of your life prior to the moment of death?" In 1 John 1:7-10 we learn that Jesus' blood continually cleanses sins (present subjunctive) if we "walk in the light" (present subjunctive) and if we "confess our sins" (present subjunctive). The present subjunctive tense in Greek implies a continuous act.[4] Jesus' blood cleanses at our baptism and it continues to cleanse after baptism as long as we continue to walk and confess. The blood of Christ does not flow from a spigot which one turns on and off. It stays on as long as we are walking and confessing as we should. We are expected to follow God's commands and to act with love (2:3; 3:16ff etc), but walking in the light includes sin (1:8-10). The issue is direction, not perfection. It is about faithfulness. John is talking about a pattern of walking and confessing.

We also need to ask if we move into and out of salvation every time we sin and repent. I cannot find biblical evidence that this is the case. It is very clear in the Bible that a person can fall from grace (Galatians 5:4; Hebrews 6:4-6). We can drive God from our lives. I can find no evidence, however, that this happens immediately with every type of sin. To begin with, we must remember that God is seeking to save us, not destroy us (2 Peter 3:9). He is not looking for an excuse to condemn us; He already had us there before the cross. Next, we need to remember that Christianity is a growth process (Ephesians 4:11-16; 2 Peter 3:17-18). We grow in our understanding of what it means to walk in the light. There are things that I now realize are wrong but was unaware of when I first became a Christian. God does not expect us to figure it out all at once.

The evidence of Christians in the New Testament who had unre-
pented sin in their lives and were still in a relationship with God proves
that one does not immediately lose salvation with every type of sin.
The church at Corinth had been guilty of numerous sins. For example,
they fellowshiped a man who was living with his father's wife and they
had corrupted the Lord's Supper (1 Corinthians 5; 11). Despite this,
Paul called them, "the Church of God," "brethren," and "saints," even
saying, "You are in Christ Jesus" (1:30). It is clear from the tone of
Paul's letters that the Corinthians needed to repent (5:1ff; 2 Corinthians
7:9), or sin would destroy their relationship with God. Yet, the relationship was not yet severed (1 Corinthians 1:4-9).

Corinth is not the only congregation we might consider. The book
of Revelation was written more than 60 years after Pentecost, and the
church at Ephesus had been in existence for more than 40 years. Every
New Testament document, except the writings of John, had been in existence for at least 25-30 years when Jesus stated the following to
Ephesus: "Remember therefore from where you have fallen; repent and
do the first works, or else I will come to you quickly and remove your
lampstand from its place – unless you repent" (Revelation 2:5). Jesus
threatened to remove their lampstand and thus to end their standing as
a congregation of His people. If they rejected Jesus' warning, they
would forfeit their relationship with Him. Because that had not oc-
curred as of the writing of the letter, the passage implies that although
sin will drive God from us, it does not happen immediately.

The final issue we must consider is, "What kind of sin was committed prior to death and was not confessed?" Why take the time to
consider this question? Because many faithful Christians live their lives
scared to death that in a moment of weakness they will make a mistake
and then be lost because they did not get a chance to repent before
death. I cannot find such teaching in God's Word.

We noted in our study of the Old Testament that God differentiated
between an unintentional sin and a "high-handed" sin (Numbers 15:25-
31). High-handed sin is rebellious sin that shakes its fist in the face
of God. Jesus spoke of the "weightier matters of the law" in Matthew
23:23. Paul also differentiated between sins. If a person was caught in
a trespass, Paul said to restore him gently (Galatians 6:1-2). Yet, when

one was living in an immoral sexual relationship he told them to "deliver such a one to Satan" (1 Corinthians 5:5). He told the elders at Crete to rebuke the false teachers "harshly" (Titus 1:13). The level of God's patience with sin seems to relate to the level of rebellion and the level of influence on others (1 Corinthians 5:6; James 3:1).

Remember that, ultimately, God makes the decision. The way to be sure of our eternal salvation is to live our lives obeying God's Word and confessing our sins. None of us should want to face God with any unconfessed sins in our lives. We do not have to live in constant fear that God is hunting for a reason to condemn us. John said, "These things I have written to you who believe in the name of the Son of God, that you may know that you have eternal life" (1 John 5:13). It is not sinful or arrogant to have confidence in your salvation. Your confidence is in Christ, not yourself.

Conclusion

A congregation conducted a survey that may shed some light on this discussion. Responses came from 167 teens and adults. Out of seven questions, the key question was, "If you died right now, would you go to heaven?" They were given four choices: Yes, No, I don't know, and I think so, but I am not sure. Of those who responded, 94 percent were Christians. Respondents were part of a Wednesday night crowd, so they would likely be among the most committed and active members. Thirty-eight percent gave one of the three negative answers. They could not say that they knew they were going to heaven. Of the teens who responded, 74 percent were unsure of their salvation (despite the fact that 74 percent of them were Christians). Amazingly, 37 percent of those in the 65 and up age group could not say they were going to heaven. These senior saints had been Christians an average of 51 years each. In the same survey, a few who had not been baptized thought that they were going to heaven. Several who never prayed or read their Bible also thought they were going to heaven.

We would likely find similar results in most congregations. So many people fail to understand what divine forgiveness is. Some fail to realize that we do not have forgiveness until we follow the biblical plan of salvation by expressing our faith in repentance, confession and bap-

tism and continue to walk in the light and confess our sins. Many fail
to realize that forgiveness involves both the release from a penalty and
the resuming of a relationship. Some focus on the release and take
for granted the relationship. They feel forgiven, yet they ignore the need
for communication, obedience and love in their relationship with God.
If there is no relationship, there is no salvation. Others focus on the relationship but doubt the release. They have a pattern of worship, prayer,
study, walking in the light and confessing sin, yet they never feel forgiven because they focus on their weaknesses rather than on His strength.
All of these people have missed the message of God's Word. They miss
the peace that forgiveness offers.

Discussion Questions

1. What would be a good one-sentence definition for forgiveness?

2. Why do you think we tend to blame others for our mistakes?

3. Do you struggle with having confidence in your salvation? Did
   anything in this chapter help?

Looking Ahead

Do you have peace? What reason or reasons do you have for your
answer?

Chapter 13

The Gift
of Peace

A visiting preacher at the Christian Chapel Church of Christ in
Hatley, Miss., began his Sunday morning sermon by asking, "Can
you sleep when the wind blows?" He then proceeded to tell the story
of Jesus sleeping during a storm on the sea of Galilee (Matthew 8:24-
27). The apostles feared for their lives while Jesus slept. He was at
peace. He was unafraid. John the apostle was present that day, and he
records in John 14 that Jesus offers that same peace to us: "Peace I
leave with you, My peace I give to you" (v. 27).

Jesus was offering a peace far greater than anything the world had
to offer. Events in the Middle East give us daily reminders of how quickly peace can be shattered. The world can never succeed in giving true
peace. The Hebrew word for peace is *shalom*. It was a common greet-
ing and farewell in the ancient world. When they wanted to ask how
someone was doing, the Jews would say, "*Hashalom lach*," meaning
"How is peace to you?" In practical usage it meant, "Is it well with
you?" Peace was a common term found in the introduction to Paul's
letters (Romans 1:7; 1 Corinthians 1:3). It was central to Jewish and
Christian thought. Jesus offered the apostles more than mere words or
greetings – He offered real peace (Philippians 4:4-7).

Jesus told the disciples at the Last Supper, "He who has My commandments and keeps them, it is he who loves Me. And he who loves

Me will be loved by My Father, and I will love him and manifest Myself to him" (John 14:21). Judas ("not Iscariot") was shocked by Jesus' statement. He thought the Messiah was to be an earthly king who would be revealed to the world. Jesus was saying He would be revealed only to the one who keeps His commandments. Judas had not expected that and asked, "Lord, how is it that You will manifest Yourself to us, and not to the world?" (v. 22).

The apostles of Jesus were about to have their worlds turned up-side down. The death of Jesus on the cross would shatter their dreams, hopes and preconceived notions about the Messiah. It would strike a great blow to their faith and courage. Jesus was offering them a peace that would aid them in the most troubling storm of their lives. Why should they have peace in the midst of the storm? If we can find out what gave them peace, then maybe we can find peace during our storms. In this lesson we will identify four reasons Jesus gave the apostles to be at peace.

Relationship With God in Christ

The peace that Jesus offered the apostles was based on a special relationship which He had enjoyed with them. Jesus did not come to be an earthly king who would rule the world from an earthly throne. He came to be a spiritual king who would reign in the hearts of those who loved Him and kept His commandments. Jesus was letting the apostles know they had something that the world did not have – a relationship with the Father and the Son. They could face the coming storm with the knowledge that they would not face it alone.

We are in a relationship with God because He atoned for our sins at the cross and forgave us at the point of baptism. Our life then is to be a life of joy and peace. Many people fail to enjoy that peace because they do not allow themselves to feel forgiven. They feel guilty for enjoying the Christian life, thinking they are supposed to be serious all the time so as to somehow make up for their mistakes. Paul called on us to "rejoice in the Lord" (Philippians 4:5). He had as much sin in his past as anyone, and he was still able to rejoice. He rejoiced not because of what he had done but because of what Christ had done for him. Paul knew that his Savior never intended for him to live in misery. He knew

Jesus came "that they may have life, and that they may have it more abundantly" (John 10:10). Allow yourself to feel forgiven and start living life more abundantly. Remember that God said of your sins, "I will remember no more" (Jeremiah 31:34).

If you seek God's forgiveness tonight and then mention the sin to Him tomorrow morning, He will not know what you are talking about. When we become Christians, God doesn't say, "Well, Johnny and Sally grew up in a Christian family so they will probably be okay, but we better watch George, we all know what he did before he became a Christian!" He forgives and forgets all our past sins, and we start on a level playing field with our slates clean. C.S. Lewis rightly noted, "If God forgives us, we must forgive ourselves. Otherwise it is almost like setting up ourselves as a higher tribunal than him."[1] One writer has stated, "Surely the only appropriate response … is an outpouring of relief and joy … . Yet, the Sunday morning response is often a glance at the bulletin to see what comes next."[2]

Some Christians fail to find joy and peace because they do not avail themselves of the blessings inherent in their relationship with the Son. They are in a relationship with God, but they try to handle their problems on their own. When Paul said, "The Lord is at hand" (Philippians 4:5), he was not talking about the second coming – he was saying that Jesus is only a prayer away (vv. 6-7). Because of the atoning sacrifice of our High Priest, we can come "boldly to the throne of grace" (Hebrews 4:14-16). Through prayer, we have access to the mercy seat where we can continue to receive forgiveness and help with our daily struggles. We find peace when we avail ourselves of this great privilege and trust our Father, who sits on the throne.

Jesus told the disciples that this relationship was contingent on their obedient love (John 14:23). Their love and knowledge were immature; they were not where they needed to be (vv. 7, 28). Despite their weaknesses, Jesus offered them peace (v. 27). He required faithfulness, not perfection. Jesus lived obedience before them so they might learn how to do likewise (v. 31; Philippians 2:5-8). As always, He practiced what He preached. We must do the same.

Because we are forgiven and are in a relationship with God, we are the temple of the Spirit (1 Corinthians 3:17; 6:19). Images of the tabernacle and the Day of Atonement should come flooding back into our minds. A holy God is in our midst, both as a church and as individual Christians. As such, we should strive to live holy lives, just as He is holy (Leviticus 11:44; 1 Peter 1:15-16). Forgiveness is not a license to sin. The biblical picture is quite the opposite. Just as the impurities of the Israelites drove God from the temple, so we can drive God from our presence if we continue in sin and rebellion. Although God is not waiting to pounce on us, He does require us to be faithful and obedient.

Remembrance of Our Relationship With God

The apostles' relationship with the Father and the Son resulted in additional help from the Holy Spirit, help that the world would not have (John 14:17, 26). The Spirit would continue to guide them and remind them of the teachings of Jesus (v. 26). There was much the apostles did not understand that the Spirit would help them comprehend. They found peace in the understanding that came from remembering the words of their Savior.

A study by the Barna Research Group stated that "93 percent of all Americans own at least one Bible, and most own more than one." A poll by George Gallup revealed that eight in 10 Americans claim to be Christians, but half do not know who preached the Sermon on the Mount. Only three out of five could name the four Gospels. The Barna study also showed that 27 percent of those who claimed to be Christians did not think there was a book of Jonah in the Bible, and 39 percent did not know that Jesus was born in Bethlehem.[3] Even in what is supposed to be a "Christian nation," people do not know the Word of God. We struggle to find peace because we are no longer a people of "The Book." We are either caught up in emotionalism, or we allow someone else to tell us what the Bible says. We do not read it for ourselves. We have made the Word of God into a museum piece. We parade through the museum each Sunday and allow the "tour guide" (the preacher) to tell us about it. Then we go home and leave the Bible at the museum. We need to study the words of the Spirit and remember what our God did to forgive us and make peace.

Return of Christ

The apostles also found peace in the return. Jesus spoke of two returns, the first referring to His return to the Father. Jesus said, "My Father is greater than I" (John 14:28). Although still divine, Jesus had lowered Himself by becoming a human being and was about to return to the glory He knew before His incarnation (17:1-4). When Jesus said, "My Father is greater," He was describing a difference in condition (human), not a difference in nature (divine). The knowledge that He was returning to His glory should have caused the apostles to rejoice. They should have found peace and joy not only in His return to the Father but also in His return from heaven to take them to the Father (14:28). He would leave glory to bring them to glory. Their separation was only temporary.

We should find peace in the reality that Jesus will return to take us into the presence of the Father (1 Thessalonians 4:17). As we noted earlier, heaven is pictured in Revelation as the Most Holy Place of the temple where we can live eternally in the very presence of God.[4] Not only will we be in the presence of God, but we will once again have access to the tree of life (Revelation 22:2). The damage done by sin will be removed. Pain, sorrow and death will be gone (21:4). We will have been forgiven and will live forever and walk with God in the new Eden as He intended from the beginning. Genesis tells of paradise lost. Revelation tells of paradise regained. Humanity's relationship with God will be fully restored in heaven.

Revealing the Future

Jesus also gave peace by revealing what would happen in the future (John 14:29). Jesus reminded the apostles that God was in control. Peter heard these words and declared on the Day of Pentecost that the events of the cross were "by the determined purpose and foreknowledge of God," but God raised Him up again (Acts 2:23-24). The Pharisees were not in charge. The Romans were not in control. Satan would not prevail. God was in charge! When the apostles faced the storm of Jesus' death, they should have remembered that Jesus had predicted it, and their faith should have grown stronger.

God is in control. Our relationship with Him is hindered by our sins, yet the will of God can never be thwarted. He has been working through-out history on the behalf of humanity. He keeps His promises. No mat-ter what storms come our way, we can know that God is working in our lives (Romans 8:28). I am a big Kentucky Wildcat basketball fan. I have a tape of a game against Duke in which we were down by 17 points with under 10 minutes left in the game, but we won! I enjoy watching the tape because I know who wins. That is the picture the Bible gives us of our future. We have joy and peace because we know who wins!

Revolutionary Living

Jesus described a peace that He offers to all His followers: "Peace I leave with you, My peace I give to you; not as the world gives do I give to you" (John 14:27). The apostle Paul declared this peace was a reality: "Therefore, having been justified by faith, we have peace with God through our Lord Jesus Christ" (Romans 5:1). In the book of Romans, Paul revealed that this peace is to permeate and revolution-ize our entire lives. Our new life in the kingdom of God is to be a life of peace, "for the kingdom of God is ... righteousness and peace and joy in the Holy Spirit" (14:17).

A life of peace changes how we view everything. Because we have peace with God, so far as it depends on us, we will seek to "live peace-ably with all men" (Romans 12:18). When it comes to our brethren, we will "pursue the things which make for peace and the things by which one may edify another" (14:19). Why? Because we are all the same. Whether Jew or Gentile, black or white, man or woman, we are all sinners in need of the forgiveness of God. We treat each other with compassion despite our mistakes because God did that for us.

Peace with God also helps us to make peace with our struggles. What problem could be worse than being the enemy of God? Because we are Christians, we are now friends of God. No matter what happens to us, we know that God is on our side (Romans 8:31). Finally, we are at peace with our guilt. We can echo the words of Paul, "O wretched man that I am! Who will deliver me from this body of death? I thank God – through Jesus Christ our Lord!" (7:24-25). No one can be perfect (3:23). Christians are not perfect, just forgiven. We are called to be faithful.

If we sacrifice truth, we sacrifice peace with God. Paul loved his nation, the Jews. He was even willing to be separated from Christ for their salvation (Romans 9:3). But he was not willing to sacrifice the message of the gospel to achieve peace with his people. We can only have peace on God's terms because He is the one wronged. He is the one who must determine how the relationship is to be repaired. Do you want a peaceful life? Then understand what it means to have peace with God. When we understand the forgiveness that makes peace possible, then we can finally become the representatives of God that He intended when He made us in His image.

Conclusion

In the summer of 1993 I stood in a hallway of the Elizabethtown Church of Christ in Elizabethtown, Ky., as a powerful storm tore the roof off over my head. I remember a feeling of total helplessness. Storms can come in many forms. It may be a financial storm or a storm of illness, a storm of death, or even a spiritual storm, but every storm that rocks our lives leaves us feeling helpless and afraid. When we face these storms, we need to remember the words of Jesus, "My peace I give to you; not as the world gives do I give to you." We have a *relationship* with the Father and the Son. The Sword of the Spirit *reminds* us of Jesus' words and love. We can know that our storms are only temporary, and He will *return* to take us home. He has also *revealed* what will happen in the future. This reality allows us to live in a revolutionary new way. We can have peace. John 20 gives us a glimpse of the aftermath of the storm of the cross. Jesus showed the apostles His hands and feet and "the disciples were glad when they saw the Lord. So Jesus said to them again, 'Peace to you!' " (vv. 20-21). The storm will pass!

We have journeyed from Genesis to Revelation and along the way we have caught a glimpse of the heart of God. We discovered a heart that reaches out to us despite our sins. I pray that as you travel the pathway of your life you will find the peace that comes through accepting the forgiveness of the Creator of the universe. I pray that your relationship with Him will sustain your darkest hours and enhance your brightest days. I challenge all of us to transplant His heart into our chests. Our world needs more people with a heart like His. Let us go forth as His representatives to help others restore their relationship with Him. I leave you with the words of Paul in Romans 15:33, "Now the God of peace be with you all. Amen."

> *"At the heart of the cyclone tearing the sky, And flinging the clouds and the towers by, Is a place of central calm; So here in the roar of mortal things, I have a place where my spirit sings, In the hollow of God's palm."* [5]

Discussion Questions

1. What is the most helpful thing you learned from this chapter? What is the most helpful thing you have learned from reading this book?

2. What is the most surprising thing you have encountered in your reading of this book?

3. Has this study accomplished what you hoped it would?

Looking Ahead

How are you going to think or act differently in the future as a result of reading this book?

Endnotes

Chapter 1

1. Rebecca Price Janney, *Great Stories in American History: A Selection of Events from the 15th to 20th Centuries* (Camp Hill, Pa.: Horizon Books, 1998) 94.
2. Sermon Illustrations, "Illustrations A-Z" 17 August 1998 eSermons.com 22 Dec. 2005 <http://www.sermonillustrations.com/illustrations_a-z.htm>.
3. *Bible Illustrator for Windows*, CD-ROM vers. 3.0e (Hiawatha: Parsons, 1998).
4. Pronunciation of Hebrew words comes from the *Strong's Exhaustive Concordance with Greek and Hebrew Dictionaries, PC Study Bible*, CD-ROM vers. 4.2 (Seattle: Biblesoft, 2004). Accented syllables in the pronunciation are in bold type (sa-lee-**kaw**).
5. *Strong's* vers. 4.2.
6. *Englishman's Hebrew Concordance of the New Testament, PC Study Bible*, CD-ROM vers. 3.2E (Seattle: Biblesoft, 2001).
7. *Strong's Exhaustive Concordance with Greek and Hebrew Dictionaries, PC Study Bible*, CD-ROM vers. 3.2E (Seattle: Biblesoft, 2001).
8. Johannes Botterweck, Helmer Ringgren, and Heinz-Josef Fabry, eds., *Theological Dictionary of the Old Testament*, vol. 10 (Grand Rapids: Eerdmans, 1986) 259.
9. *Vine's Expository Dictionary of Biblical Words, PC Study Bible*, CD-ROM vers. 3.2E (Seattle: Biblesoft, 2001).
10. The single quotation mark (') represents the silent Hebrew letter *aleph* when transliterating Hebrew words into English (cf. *nasa'*).
11. *Brown, Driver and Briggs' Hebrew-English Lexicon, PC Study Bible*, CD-ROM vers. 3.2E (Seattle: Biblesoft, 2001).
12. Botterweck, Ringgren, and Fabry 25.
13. Botterweck, Ringgren, and Fabry 31.
14. *International Standard Bible Encyclopaedia, PC Study Bible*, CD-ROM vers. 3.2E (Seattle: Biblesoft, 2001).
15. *Englishman's Hebrew Concordance.*
16. *Brown, Driver and Briggs.*
17. Another related term is *kacah* (kaw-**saw**). This word is usually used with the literal meaning of "to cover." For example, the pillar of cloud is said to have covered (*kacah*) the tabernacle in Numbers 9:16. Yet, in a few places it is used with the sense of "forgive" (*Theological Wordbook of the Old Testament, PC Study Bible*, CD-ROM vers. 4.2). One example is Psalm 32:1 where it is used in connection with *nasa'*; "Blessed is he whose transgression is forgiven [*nasa'*], whose sin is covered [*kacah*]" (*Englishman's Hebrew Concordance*). *Brown, Driver and Briggs' Hebrew-English Lexicon* states that *kacah* means "to cover, conceal, to hide."
18. James L. Mays, quoted by Claire Vonk Brooks, "Between Text and Sermon: Psalm 51," *Interpretation* 99 (January 1995): 63.
19. *Interlinear Transliterated Bible, PC Study Bible*, CD-ROM vers. 3.2E (Seattle: Biblesoft, 2001).
20. *Strong's* vers. 3.2E.
21. *Keil and Delitzsch Commentary on the Old Testament, PC Study Bible*, CD-ROM vers. 3.2E (Seattle: Biblesoft, 2001).

22. *Interlinear Transliterated Bible.*
23. *Interlinear Transliterated Bible.*
24. *Strong's* vers. 3.2E.
25. *Keil and Delitzsch.*
26. *Brown, Driver and Briggs.*
27. *Englishman's Hebrew Concordance.*
28. Claire Vonk Brooks, "Between Text and Sermon: Psalm 51," *Interpretation* 99 (January 1995): 63.
29. Botterweck, Ringgren, and Fabry 35.
30. *Bible Illustrator.*

Chapter 2
1. John Bonnett Wexo, ZooBooks: Snakes (San Diego: Wildlife Education Ltd., 2001).
2. *Theological Wordbook of the Old Testament.*
3. Stanley J. Grenz, *Theology for the Community of God* (Grand Rapids: Eerdmans, 1994) 174.
4. Alfred Edersheim, *Bible History: Old Testament* (Grand Rapids: Eerdmans, 1987) 184.

Chapter 3
1. Thomas Raitt, "Why Does God Forgive?," *Horizons in Biblical Theology* 13 (June 1991): 38.
2. Raitt 39.
3. *Brown, Driver and Briggs.*
4. *Englishman's Hebrew Concordance.*
5. *Englishman's Hebrew Concordance.*
6. Botterweck, Ringgren, and Fabry 34.
7. *Englishman's Hebrew Concordance.*
8. *Englishman's Hebrew Concordance.*
9. *Nasa'* is used to mean "forgive" twice in Isaiah and once in Micah. *Calach* is found once in Isaiah, seven times in Jeremiah and Lamentations, once in Daniel, and once in Amos (*Englishman's Hebrew Concordance*).
10. Raitt 40.
11. Paul R. House, *Old Testament Theology* (Downers Grove: InterVarsity, 1998) 206.
12. *Keil and Delitzsch.*
13. Wayne Jackson, *A Study Guide to Greater Bible Knowledge* (Stockton, CA: Apologetics Press, 1986) 10.
14. Dallas Willard, *The Divine Conspiracy: Rediscovering Our Hidden Life in God* (San Francisco: Harper, 1998) 1.
15. Edward C. Wharton, *The Scheme of Redemption* (Lubbock, TX: Sunset, 1972) 13.

Chapter 4
1. "United States Secret Service: Protection" 22 Dec. 2005 <http://www.secretservice.gov/protection_works.shtml>.

2. R.K. Harrison, *Leviticus: An Introduction and Commentary*, Tyndale Old Testament Comm. (Downers Grove: InterVarsity, 1981) 166.

3. Jacob Milgrom, *Leviticus 1-16, The Anchor Bible* (New York: Doubleday, 1991) 1013.

4. Gordon J. Wenham, *The Book of Leviticus, The New International Commentary on the Old Testament* (Grand Rapids: Eerdmans, 1979) 228.

5. *Brown, Driver and Briggs.*

6. *Englishman's Greek Concordance of the New Testament, PC Study Bible*, CD-ROM vers. 3.2E (Seattle: Biblesoft, 2001).

7. Cf. Baruch A. Levine, *The JPS Torah Commentary: Leviticus* (Philadelphia: The Jewish Publication Society, 1989) 100.

8. Cf. Harrison 169.

9. J.R. Porter, *Leviticus*, The Cambridge Bible Commentary (New York: Cambridge Press, 1976) 126.

10. *Keil and Delitzsch.*

11. Wenham 230.

12. Cf. Harrison 169.

13. Wenham 88-89.

14. Wenham 51-57.

15. Cf. Levine 101.

16. Cf. Porter 127. For another possibility see Milgrom 1019-20 and compare Yoma 4:1-2 of Jacob Neusner's translation of *The Mishnah,* 270-71.

17. Jacob Neusner, *The Mishnah* (New Haven: Yale P, 1988) 270.

18. See Levine 102 and Milgrom 1020-21.

19. Neusner 275.

20. See Levine 102; Milgrom 1020-21; and Jacqueline C.R. De Roo, "Was the Goat for Azazel Destined for the Wrath of God?," *Biblica* 81 (August 2000): 233-242.

21. Of these three possibilities, the first carries the least weight. The second rendering, "for Azazel," has strengths, but its weaknesses are weightier. Laird Harris notes that the book of 1 Enoch is dependent on Leviticus 16 rather than vice versa and is therefore of no value in interpreting *azazel*. Harris also says the argument stating that "for Azazel" creates an exact parallel to "for the Lord" presses the grammatical parallel too far. He further notes a similar cleansing ritual in Leviticus 14:7 with no evidence of "demonology" being connected with that ritual (R. Laird Harris, "Leviticus," *Genesis-Numbers*, The Expositor's Bible Commentary vol. 2, Frank E. Gaebelein, ed. Grand Rapids: Regency, 1990. 590). If *azazel* refers to a demon, the Israelites would likely view the goat as an offering to the demon (especially in light of the parallel with the goat "for the Lord"), which would seem to pay homage to the demon and as such would contradict the statement in Leviticus 17:7 (cf. Wenham 88-89 and Harrison 170-171).

22. Harrison 170.

Chapter 5

1. "Tribute to Bobby Ray Memorial Elementary School (Senate – October 10, 1995)" The Library of Congress THOMAS 22 Dec. 2005 <http://thomas.loc.gov/cgi-bin/query/D?r104:3:./temp/~r104EMxZAv::>.

2. Cf. Wenham 231.

3. Levine 105.

4. *International Standard Bible Encyclopaedia.*

5. Levine 105.

6. *Englishman's Greek Concordance.*

7. Cf. Wenham 28.

8. M.C. Sansom, "Laying on of Hands in the Old Testament," *The Expository Times* 94 (August 1983): 323-26.

9. Neusner 275.

10. Porter 131.

11. Porter 131.

12. Harrison 174.

13. Harrison 174-175.

14. Cf. Harris 591.

16. John E. Hartley, *Word Biblical Commentary: Leviticus* (Dallas: Word Books, 1992) 246.

Chapter 6

1. Robert Saucy, *Scripture: Its Power, Authority, and Relevance* (Nashville: Word, 2001) 110.

2. Terry Briley, Class handout, Theology of the Old Testament (Nashville: Lipscomb University, 2003).

3. The accent in pronunciation is denoted by boldface type.

4. *Englishman's Greek Concordance.*

5. *Strong's* vers. 3.2E.

6. Gerhard Kittel and Gerhard Friedrich., eds. *Theological Dictionary of the New Testament,* abridged by Geoffrey W. Bromiley, Logos Library System, New Testament Greek Core Collection, CD-ROM (Oak Harbor: Logos, 1997).

7. Joseph Henry Thayer, *A Greek-English Lexicon of the Greek New Testament, PC Study Bible,* CD-ROM vers. 3.2E (Seattle: Bible Soft, 2001).

8. *Englishman's Greek Concordance.*

9. *International Standard Bible Encyclopaedia.*

10. *Robertson's New Testament Word Pictures, PC Study Bible*, CD-ROM vers. 3.2E (Seattle: Biblesoft, 2001).

11. Kittel and Friedrich.

12. Kittel and Friedrich.

13. Thayer.

14. *Vine's.*

15. *Vine's.*

16. *Strong's* vers. 3.2E.

17. Thayer.

18. *International Standard Bible Encyclopaedia.*

19. Thayer.

20. *International Standard Bible Encyclopaedia.*

21. *Englishman's Greek Concordance.*

22. Thayer.

23. Joel B. Green, *New Testament Theology: The Theology of the Gospel of Luke* (Cambridge: Cambridge P, 1995) 2.
24. Kittel and Friedrich.

Chapter 7
1. Green 76-77.
2. Green 76-77.
3. *Englishman's Greek Concordance.*
4. Sermon Illustrations.
5. "Nobel Peace Prize Laureates," The Nobel Peace Prize 17 Aug. 1998 The Norwegian Nobel Institute 31 Oct. 2005 <http://www.nobel.no/eng_lau_list.html>.
6. Walter Bauer, *A Greek-English Lexicon of the New Testament and Other Early Christian Literature*, W.F. Arndt and F.W. Gingrich trans. and eds. from Bauer's 4th ed. 1949-52, 9th impression 1965 (Chicago: Univ. of Chicago P, 1957) 197.
7. *Bible Illustrator.*

Chapter 8
1. Ray Boltz, "Watch the Lamb" from the album "Watch the Lamb" (Muncie, IN: Ray Boltz Ministries, 1986).
2. Wenham 28.
3. Steve Stanley, "Hebrews 9:6-10: The 'Parable' of the Tabernacle," *Novum Testamentum* 37 (October 1995): 394.
4. Terry Briley, "The Old Testament 'Sin Offering' and Christ's Atonement," *Stone-Campbell Journal* 3 (Spring 2000): 90-93.
5. Hartley 246.
6. *Bible Illustrator.*

Chapter 9
1. Thomas R. Schreiner, *Interpreting the Pauline Epistles* (Grand Rapids: Baker, 1990) 43.
2. Schreiner 43.
3. Donald Guthrie, *New Testament Introduction*, 3rd ed. 1970 (Downers Grove: InterVarsity, 1965) 546-50; Everett F. Harrison, *Introduction to the New Testament* (Grand Rapids: Eerdmans, 1964) 324-35; F.F. Bruce, *The Epistle to the Ephesians* (London: Revell, 1961) 14.
4. cf. Bruce 14.
5. "USS *Arizona* History" 22 Dec. 2005 <http://www.pearlharbor.org/center-ships-uss-arizona.asp>.
6. *Englishman's Greek Concordance.*
7. Jack Cottrell, *God the Redeemer* (Joplin: College P, 1987) 15-17.
8. Thayer.
9. N.T. Wright, *Colossians and Philemon,* Tyndale New Testament Commentaries (Grand Rapids: Eerdmans, 1999) 63.
10. Thayer.

11. Jeannine Clegg, "The Flag raising was 'shot in the arm,' " September11News.com 22 Dec. 2005 <http://www.september11news.com/FDNYFireman.htm>.

Chapter 10

1. Janney 94-100.
2. *Englishman's Greek Concordance.*
3. For further study, see Jack Cottrell, *Baptism and the Remission of Sins*, David W. Fletcher, ed. (Joplin:College P, 1990) 16, 68-73.
4. J.D. Thomas, *Romans,* The Living Word Commentaries (Austin: Sweet, 1965) 32.
5. *International Standard Bible Encyclopaedia.*
6. *Bible Illustrator.*

Chapter 11

1. *Bible Illustrator.*
2. cf. *The Word in Life Study Bible: NKJV* (Nashville: Thomas Nelson, 1996) 1675.
3. cf. David Roper. *The Life of Christ, Truth for Today Commentary Series* (Searcy, AR: Resource, 2003) 582.
4. Jess Hall, Jr. "Preaching – Illustrating the Sermon." Nov. 1997 *Firm Foundation* 31 Oct. 2005 <www.bible-infonet.org/ff/articles/preaching/112_11_01.htm>.
5. *The Word in Life Study Bible* 1675.
6. *Bible Illustrator.*
7. *Bible Illustrator.*
8. *Bible Illustrator.*
9. *Bible Illustrator.*

Chapter 12

1. *UBS New Testament Handbook Series, PC Study Bible*, CD-ROM vers. 3.2E (Seattle: Biblesoft, 2001).
2. *Bible Illustrator.*
3. Pettus Read, "Whose Fault Is It Anyway?," *Tennessee Connections* (May 2001): 4.
4. Cf. William Mounce, *Basics of Biblical Greek* (Grand Rapids: Zondervan, 1993) 283.

Chapter 13

1. *Bible Illustrator.*
2. Brooks 55.
3. Sermon Illustrations.
4. Terry Briley, Class notes.
5. Edwin Markham, *Bible Illustrator.*

9 780892 255535